That's My King!

Your eyes will behold the King in
His beauty . . . Isaiah 33:17

That's My King!

Meditations on the Christ Who is All in All

Joseph Randall

ISBN: 1500616419
ISBN-13: 978-1500616410

Resources To Help You Trust And Delight In King Jesus

1. "That's My King!"
   https://www.youtube.com/watch?v=wUDgBNhKBME

2. Desiring God: http://www.desiringgod.org/

3. 9 Marks: http://9marks.org/

4. The Gospel Coalition:
   http://www.thegospelcoalition.org/

5. Ligonier Ministries: http://www.ligonier.org/

6. Charles Spurgeon: http://www.spurgeon.org/

7. Monergism: http://www.monergism.com/

8. Grace To You: http://www.gty.org/

DEDICATION

Charles Spurgeon, the great London preacher, was once told by his grandfather that he might preach the Gospel better than his grandfather does, but he could not preach a better Gospel!

In that same spirit I write: many people write better poetry than I do (maybe everyone!), but none write poetry about a better Subject, Object, Focus, Topic, Friend, or Lover. Jesus Christ is the Alpha and Omega of this poetry! He's the Beginning and the End of this poetry! He's the First and the Last of this poetry! And it is to Him, His Father, and His Spirit, and to Them alone I dedicate this book.

To my KING:

"Whom have I in heaven but You? And there is nothing on earth that I desire besides You." Psalm 73:25

"If anyone comes to Me and does not hate his own father and mother and wife and children and brothers and sisters, yes, and even his own life, he cannot be My disciple." Jesus in Luke 14:26

Jesus Christ You are my King of kings and my Lord of lords!

You are the most beautiful. There is no one like You!

"Long as I got King Jesus, I don't need nobody else!" Vickie Winans

"Your eyes will behold the King in His beauty . . . ." Isaiah 33:17

"One thing have I asked of the LORD, that will I seek after – to gaze upon the beauty of the LORD . . . ." Psalm 27:4

NO KING BUT CHRIST!

A Hymn to my King

CHRIST IS ALL!
Tune: Come Thou Fount

Whom have I in heav'n but You LORD
You are everything to me!
You're my King, my LORD, my Savior
From my idols set me free!
Make me hope in You alone LORD
Be the "Christ is all!" to me!
Come and capture my whole being
And Your beauty let me see!

Nothing on earth I desire LORD
Save for You and You alone!
At the cross Your great love out poured
Sent Your Son Who did atone!
Then He rose up with all power
Conquered hell, sin, pain, and death!
Now His name is my strong tower
To Him run, and you'll find rest!

I am weak – I have no power
LORD! I don't know what to do!
But my eyes are ever on You
Father come and lead me through!
You're my God Who has all power
There is nothing You can't do!
Come and save now – Spirit lead me
Grant me mercy pure and true!

Those who seek You lack no good thing
For in Christ we have it all!
You're all beauty; You're all glory
You're the God-Man; You're our all!
You alone are satisfaction
You're the pleasure of our life!
Come oh LORD now be our Treasure
Be our Joy and our Delight!

CONTENTS

CHRIST IS ALL!

ACKNOWLEDGMENTS

"Trust in the LORD with all your heart, and do not lean on your own understanding. In all your ways acknowledge Him, and He will make straight your paths."
Proverbs 3:5-6

"Let the one who boasts, boast in the Lord."
1 Corinthians 1:31

"But far be it from me to boast except in the cross of our Lord Jesus Christ, by which the world has been crucified to me, and I to the world." Galatians 6:14

"Here there is not Greek and Jew, circumcised and uncircumcised, barbarian, Scythian, slave, free; but Christ is all, and in all." Colossians 3:11

"For we are powerless against this great horde that is coming against us. We do not know what to do, but our eyes are on You." 2 Chronicles 20:12

"Your eyes will behold the King in His beauty" Isaiah 33:17

Thank You – Father, Son, and Holy Spirit – You are all in all. I thank God for my family, my church family, my friends, and the many godly pastors and mentors God has given me and used throughout my life to mold and shape me into what He wants me to be today. There's so much more work to be done! Thank you, Olney Baptist Church, for your love and support. It was in the midst of ministry from you and to you that this book was born. May it provoke you to delight in your King all the more!

Christ is all!

Joseph Randall
Philadelphia, Pennsylvania

She said no
So he would firm and deeply know
That Christ is all and all let go
And in the low this truth would grow
And Christ's great blessings ever flow
For when you praise Him in the low
His greatest value you will show
So "Christ is all!" – all else forgo
Now He is all I need I know!
That's my King!

May King Jesus be our Preoccupation, Infatuation, and
holy Fascination, for He causes intoxication more
than anything else in all of creation!

Joseph Randall

And oh, what a fair One, what an only One, what an
excellent, lovely, ravishing One, is Jesus! Put the beauty of
ten thousand worlds of paradises, like the garden of Eden
in one; put all trees, all flowers, all smells, all colors, all
tastes, all joys, all sweetness, all loveliness, in one: oh,
what a fair and excellent thing would that be! And yet it
would be less to that fair and dearest Well-beloved, Christ,
than one drop of rain to the whole seas, rivers, lakes, and
fountains of ten thousand earths. Oh, but Christ is
heaven's wonder, and earth's wonder! What marvel that
His bride saith, "He is altogether lovely!"

Samuel Rutherford

I see a man cannot be a faithful minister, until he
preaches Christ for Christ's sake – until he gives up
striving to attract people to himself, and seeks
only to attract them to Christ.

Robert Murray M'Cheyne

1
S. M. LOCKRIDGE AND "THAT'S MY KING!"

Dr. Shadrach Meshach Lockridage was the pastor of Calvary Baptist Church in San Diego, CA, for over forty years. He died and went to be with his King Jesus on April 4, 2000. Under Jesus Christ, his preaching has been the inspiration for this book.

In a sermon on the word "Amen" from the Lord's prayer, Dr. Lockridge broke out into a glorious description of the Lord Jesus Christ known as "That's My King!"[1] Outside the Bible, it is the most glorious, powerful, amazing, beautiful, wonderful description of Jesus Christ I have ever read or heard. Nothing outside the Bible, prayer, and the local church has helped me fight depression, loneliness, sadness, self-pity, selfishness, fear, anxiety, and all manner of other sins more than this glorious description of Jesus Christ. It has helped me fix my eyes on Jesus – "the Founder and Perfecter of our faith" (Hebrews 12:2) – like almost nothing else!

---

1   You can listen to the full version of the sermon here: S. M. Lockridge, "Amen" https://www.youtube.com/watch?v=2iJtfM8FVgg Accessed 01 JAN 2015.

CHRIST IS ALL!

It is this description of Jesus Christ that has inspired me to write more descriptions of Him in the same spirit and style as Dr. Lockridge. I have written them based on books of the Bible, based on special occasions, with rhymes, and based on Bible passages as I've preached through the Gospel of Mark. May God use this book to do what Dr. Lockridge said every sermon ought to do:

1. Instruct the mind (teach more knowledge about God)
2. Warm the heart (cause deep delight in God)
3. Move the will (encourage holy action for God's glory)
4. And tan your hide (convict of sin)

A Prayer Of Consecration As We Read

Oh Father, we praise and thank You that You are the most beautiful reality in the universe! You, above all, are worthy of poetry and love songs! We praise You that You are all beauty and glory and that You created all things for Your glory! We praise You for Your Son Jesus Christ! Thank You for creating Dr. S. M. Lockridge, and thank You for saving him and for filling him with faith in and love for the Lord Jesus Christ Who is King of kings and LORD of lords! Thank You for the description of King Jesus that You gave to him. May You be pleased to continue to use it and the rest of this book to point many people to Christ! May You use it to glorify Yourself, build up and help Your Church, save sinners, help the most poor, needy, and helpless, and conform Your people into the image of Jesus! As we read the poetry in this book, please open our eyes by the power of Your Holy Spirit to see His beauty and cause us to be satisfied with Him as we never have been before! Please fill our minds with glorious truths about You! May we see the King in His beauty! Please warm our hearts to delight in You as we've never delighted in You before! Please move us to act in all our ways to bring You the glory due Your name! Please convict us of our sin in all areas we need conviction! Please cause us to taste and see that You are good! Please open our eyes that we might behold wonderful truths about You! Please satisfy us with Your

2

mercy that we might be joyful in You all our days! Please fill us with Your Holy Spirit and cause us to bear lasting fruit! Please cause us to know the height and width and length and depth of the love of Christ which surpasses knowledge, and please fill us with all Your fullness oh Father, by the power of your Spirit, for Jesus' sake! Amen!

Here is Dr. Lockridge's glorious description of King Jesus![2]

That's My King!

Whoever heard of a Kingdom without a King?

Everybody's got a King!

Who is your King?

If when I ask you "Who is your King?" – you ask me Who is mine.

You got a minute?

My King is the only One qualified to be King!

My King has always been King!

You know these other Kings, they were born a prince and had to wait till their father died or their mother, if she was the ruling monarch, wait until she died and then become king!

But my King was born King!

---

2   You really must listen to them! Two of my favorite versions of "That's My King!" on the web can be found here:

1. http://www.godtube.com/watch/?v=9EJ92MNU

2. https://www.youtube.com/watch?v=wUDgBNhKBME

Accessed 01 JAN 2015.

CHRIST IS ALL!

In fact the Bible says He's a Seven Way King!
He's the King of the Jews – that's an ethnic King!
He's the King of Israel – that's a national King!
My King will let you know who's who and what's what!
My King always has been King and always will be King!

He's the King of righteousness!
He's the King of the ages!
He's the King of heaven!
He's the King of glory!
He's the King of kings,!
And He is the Lord of lords!

Now that's my King!

Well David said the heavens declare the glory of God, and
the firmament showeth His handiwork!

That's my King!

My King is the only One of Whom there are no means of
measure that can define His limitless love!

My King is a sovereign King!

No far seeing telescope can bring into visibility the
coastline of His shoreless supplies!

That's my King!

Nobody can keep Him from saving me!
I don't care what you tell Him about me – He knows me!
No barrier can hinder Him from pouring out His blessing!

He's enduringly strong!
He's entirely sincere!
He's eternally steadfast!
He's immortally graceful!
He's imperially powerful!
He's impartially merciful!

CHRIST IS ALL!

He's the greatest Phenomenon that has ever crossed the horizon of this world!
He's God's Son!
He's the sinner's Savior!
He's the Centerpiece of civilization!

That's my King!

What I like about Him – He doesn't need me, and He doesn't need you!
He stands alone in Himself!
He's august!
He's unique!
He's unparalleled!
He's unprecedented!
He's supreme!
He's preeminent!
He's the loftiest Idea in literature!
He's the highest Personality in philosophy!
He's the supreme Problem in higher criticism!
He's the fundamental Doctrine of true theology!
He's the cardinal Necessity of spiritual religion!
He's the only One qualified to be an all sufficient Savior!

That's my King!

He's the Miracle of the age!
He's the Superlative of everything good that you choose to call Him!
He's in every way able to satisfy every need – your need and mine!
He's the only One able to supply all of our needs simultaneously!
He can hear all of us pray at the same time!
He supplies strength for the weak!
He's available for the tempted and the tried!
He sympathizes, and He saves!
He's the Almighty God Who guides and keeps all His people!
He heals the sick!

CHRIST IS ALL!

He cleanses the lepers!
He forgives sinners!
He discharges debtors!
He delivers the captives!
He defends the feeble!
He blesses the young!
He serves the unfortunate!
He regards the aged!
He rewards the diligent, and He beautifies the meek!

Now that's my King! Well! Do you know Him?!

Do you know Him?! Do you know Him?!

That's my King!

My King is the Key to knowledge!
He's the Wellspring of wisdom!
He's the Doorway of deliverance!
He's the Pathway of peace!
He's the Roadway of righteousness!
He's the Highway of holiness!
He's the Gateway of glory!
He's the Master of the mighty!
He's the Captain of the conquerors!
He's the Head of the heroes!
He's the Leader of the legislators!
He's the Overseer of the overcomers!
He's the Governor of governors!
He's the Prince of princes!
He's the King of kings, and He's the Lord of lords!

That's my King! Is He yours?!

What I like about Him . . .

His office is manifold!
His promise is sure!
His light is matchless!
His goodness is limitless!

CHRIST IS ALL!

His mercy is everlasting!
His love never changes!
His Word is enough!
His grace is sufficient!
His reign is righteous!
His yoke is easy, and His burden is light!

I wish I could describe Him to you, but He's indescribable!

He's indescribable!
He's incomprehensible!
He's invincible!
He's irresistible!
I'm trying to tell you, the heaven of heavens cannot contain
Him, let alone a man explain Him!
You can't get Him out of your mind!
You can't get Him off of your hand!
You can't outlive Him, and you can't live without Him!

That's my King!

The Pharisees couldn't stand Him, but they found out they
couldn't stop Him!
Pilate couldn't find any fault in Him!
The witnesses couldn't get their testimonies to agree about
Him!
Herod couldn't kill Him!
Death couldn't handle Him!
And the grave couldn't hold Him!

That's my King!

He always has been, and He always will be!
I'm talking about He had no predecessor, and He'll have no
successor!
There was nobody before Him, and there'll be nobody after
Him!
You can't impeach Him, and He's not gonna resign!

That's my King! That's my King!

He must increase, but I must decrease.

John 3:30

Sir, we wish to see Jesus.

John 12:21

. . . and now many a sweet, sweet, soft kiss, many perfumed, well-smelled kisses, and embracements have I received of my royal Master. He and I have had much love together. I have for the present a sick [diminishing] life, with much pain, and much love-sickness for Christ. Oh, what would I give to have a bed made to my wearied soul, in His bosom! I would [delay] heaven for many years to have my fill of Jesus in this life, and to have occasion to offer Christ to my people, and to woo many people to Christ. I cannot tell you what sweet pain, and delightsome torments are in Christ's love . . . I profess to you, I have no rest, I have no ease, while I be over head and ears in love's ocean. If Christ's love (that fountain of delight) were laid as open to me as I would wish, oh, how I would drink, and drink abundantly! Oh how drunken would this my soul be!

Samuel Rutherford

2
"THAT'S MY KING!"
IN THE BOOK OF HEBREWS!

My King is God's final Word to His people; and though heaven and earth will pass away, His Words shall never pass away!

He's the heir of all things!
Through Him God created the world!
He's the Radiance of the glory of God!
He's the exact Imprint of God's nature!
He upholds the universe by the word of His power!

That's my King! I wonder if you know Him today?!

After making purification for sins, He sat down at the right hand of majesty on high!
He's superior to the angels!
His name is more excellent than all the names of the most wonderful angels!
He's worshiped by angels!

CHRIST IS ALL!

In fact, angels – angels who have worshiped at the very throne room of God Almighty for centuries – they long to look into the redemption which my King has accomplished for His people!

His Father says to Him: "Your throne, O God is forever and ever!"
He loves righteousness!
He hates wickedness!
He laid the foundations of the earth in the beginning!
The heavens are the work of His hands!
Heaven and earth will perish, but He will remain!
Heaven and earth will wear out like a garment, but He is the same yesterday, today, and forever!
His years have no end!

That's my King!

He's crowned with glory!
He's crowned with honor!
He tasted death for everyone!
Through death He destroyed the one who has the power of death – the Devil!
He's the deliverer of all those enslaved by the fear of death!
He helps the offspring of Abraham!
He's the merciful and faithful high priest!
He's the wrath bearing sacrifice for His people!
He endured temptation that He might help those who are tempted!

That's my King! Do you know Him?!

He's the Apostle and High Priest of our confession!
He's absolutely faithful to God, like no other who has ever lived!
He's worthy of more glory than Moses!
He built the house, and He Who builds all things is God!
He's a great high priest Who passed through the heavens!
He sympathizes with our weaknesses!
He was tempted in every respect as we are, yet without sin!

CHRIST IS ALL!

He made a way for us to draw near to the throne of grace with confidence that we may receive mercy and find grace to help in time of need!

That's my King!

He's a priest forever, after the order of Melchizedek!
He offered up prayers to God with tears and loud cries and was heard because of His reverence!
He became the source of eternal salvation to all who obey Him!
He's our hope – the sure and steadfast anchor of our souls!
He entered into the inner place behind the curtain as a forerunner on our behalf to bring us back to God!
He's the King of righteousness!
He's the King of peace!
He had no beginning of days, and He has no end of life!

That's my King!

He's the Lion of the tribe of Judah, and when He roars, all the beasts of field are silent!
He became an eternal priest by the power of an indestructible life!
He introduced a better hope through which we draw near to God!
He guarantees to us a better covenant!
He holds His priesthood permanently because He continues forever!
He's able to save to the uttermost all those who draw near to God through Him!
He always lives to make intercession for all His children!

That's my King! I wonder if you know Him today?!

He's High Priest!
He's holy!
He's innocent!
He's unstained!
He's separated from sinners!

CHRIST IS ALL!

He's exalted above the heavens!
He has no needs!
He has no weaknesses anymore!
He's perfect forever!

That's my King!

He's seated at the right hand of the throne of the Majesty in heaven!
He's a Minister in the holy places!
His ministry is much more excellent than the old covenant!
He's the Mediator of a better covenant enacted on better promises!
He entered once for all into the holy places by His own blood to secure eternal redemption!
Through the eternal Spirit He offered Himself to God without blemish!

That's my King!

Only His blood can purify our conscience from dead works to serve the living God!
He's the Mediator of a new covenant, so that we may receive the promised eternal inheritance!
His death is the only death that redeems from the sins committed under the first covenant!
He entered into heaven itself in the presence of God on our behalf!
He has appeared once for all at the end of the ages to put away sin by the sacrifice of Himself!
He will appear a second time, not to deal with sin, but to save those who are eagerly waiting for Him!

Are you eagerly waiting for Your King's return today?!

He's the Reality of realities of the all the good things to come!
He came to do God's will, and He's the only One Who did it perfectly!
He offered for all time a single sacrifice for sins!

CHRIST IS ALL!

He sat down at the right hand of God!
All His enemies shall be made a footstool for His feet!
By a single offering He has perfected for all time those who
are being sanctified!
He gives us confidence to enter the holy places by His own
shed blood!
He opened for us a new and living way to draw near to
God!
He's worthy for us to endure all manner of persecution for
the sake of His name!

That's my King!

He's the Founder and Perfecter of our faith!
For the joy set before Him, He endured the cross!
He's seated at the right hand of the throne of God!
He endured the hostility of sinners and prevailed mightily!
His blood speaks a better word to us than the blood of
Abel!
He's the same yesterday, today, and forever!
He suffered outside the gate in order to sanctify the people
through His own blood!
He's worthy of our continual sacrifice of praise!
He's the great Shepherd of the sheep!
His blood is the blood of the eternal covenant!

That's My King! Do you know Him?!

He's better than all our fathers!
He's better than all the prophets!
He's better than all the priests!
He's better than all the kings!
He's better than all the angels!
He's better than Adam!
He's better than Noah!
He's better than Job!
He's better than Abraham!
He's better than Joseph!
He's better than Moses!
He's better than Joshua!

CHRIST IS ALL!

He's better than David!
He's better than Daniel!
He's better than the old covenant!
He's better than all the sacrifices!
He's better than anything before Him or after Him!
He's better than anything you can dream or imagine!
He's better than the best of the best and whatever is better
that you can think of!
To Him be all glory forever and ever! Amen!

That's my King! That's my King!

Convene all your lovers before your soul, and give them their leave; and strike hands with Christ, that thereafter there may be no happiness to you but Christ, no hunting for anything but Christ, no bed at night, when death cometh, but Christ. Christ, Christ, who but Christ!

Samuel Rutherford

Looking unto Jesus – three words only, but in these three words is the whole secret of life. Looking unto Jesus in the Scriptures to learn Who He is, what He has done, why He did it, and where He is now. Looking unto Jesus incarnate, our Representative, our federal Head and Surety. Looking unto Jesus crucified, to find in His blood our ransom, our pardon, our peace. Looking unto Jesus risen again, to find in Him the righteousness which alone justifies us and permits us, unworthy as we are, to approach with assurance in His name, Him Who is His Father and our Father, His God and our God. Looking unto Jesus glorified, to find in Him our High Priest, our heavenly advocate, appearing even now for us before the presence of God and supplying the imperfections of our persons and prayers by the efficacy of His holiness and His prayers, which the Father hears always. Looking unto Jesus and not to our faith, for it is not of faith that strength comes, but it is from the Savior by faith. It is not looking unto our look: it is by looking unto Jesus. Looking unto Jesus and not to our strength nor our weakness, not to our gifts nor our griefs, not to our meditations or lack of them, not to our brethren nor our enemies. It is looking unto Jesus ALONE, unto Jesus AGAIN, unto Jesus ALWAYS, and unto Jesus UNTIL He comes again and "we shall be like Him for we shall see Him as He is."

Adolphe Monod

3
"THAT'S MY KING!"
WHO IS THE ALL IN ALL GOD-MAN!

He saved His people by His blood, and He Who saved His people by His blood is God!
He's the Bridegroom, and the Bridegroom is God!
He gives life to the dead, and He Who gives life to the dead is God!
He's worshiped by angels, and He Who's worshiped by angels is God!
He's the Almighty, and the Almighty is God!
He's addressed in prayer, and He Who's addressed in prayer is God!
He's the Light, and the Light is God!
He's the great I AM, and the great I AM is God!
His Word stands forever, and the Word that stands forever is God's!
He's the Word, and the Word is God!
He's the Holy One, and the Holy One is God!
He calmed the storming seas, and the storming seas are calmed by God!
He's the I AM He, and the I AM He is God!

That's my King! I wonder if you know Him today?!

CHRIST IS ALL!

He's the First and the Last, and the First and the Last is God!
He's the Alpha and the Omega, and the Alpha and the Omega is God!
He's the Beginning and the End, and the Beginning and the End is God!
He's the Rock, and the Rock is God!
He's the One Husband, and the One Husband is God!
He's the One Master, and the One Master is God!
He's the Lord of Lords, and the Lord of Lords is God!
He's the One Shepherd, and the One Shepherd is God!
He's the One Savior, and the One Savior is God!
He's the One Redeemer, and the One Redeemer is God!
He's the Worthy One, and the Worthy One is God!
He receives glory, honor, and power; and glory, honor, and power are received by God!
He's the Lord and God, and the Lord and God is God!
He alone must be worshiped and adored, and He alone Who must be worshiped and adored is God!

That's my King!

He's the Wonderful Counselor, and He Who is wonderful in counsel is God!
He's the Mighty God, and the Mighty God is God!
He's everlasting, and He Who is everlasting is God!
His throne is forever and ever, and He Whose throne is forever and ever is God!
He built the house, and He Who built all things is God!
He's the God over all, and the God over all is God!
He raised Himself from the dead, and He Who raised Jesus from the dead is God!
He dwells in believers, and He Who dwells in believers is God!
He sanctifies believers, and He Who sanctifies believers is God!
He searches the heart of man, and He Who searches the heart of man is God!
He owns all believers as His own, and He Who owns all believers as His own is God!

CHRIST IS ALL!

He reigns over believers as slaves, and He Who reigns over believers as slaves is God!
He's the great God, and the great God is God!

That's my King!

He had a way prepared for Him, and a way was prepared for God!
He's the LORD our righteousness, and the LORD our righteousness is God!
His is the only name you can and must call upon to be saved, and the only name you can and must call upon to be saved is God's!
Every knee must and will bow only to Him, and every knee must and will bow only to God!
He's present everywhere, and He Who is present everywhere is God!
He searches minds and hearts and knows all things, and He Who searches minds and hearts and knows all things is God!
He's the same yesterday, today, and forever and does not change, and He Who is the same yesterday, today, and forever and does not change is God!
In Him dwells the fullness of deity bodily, and the fullness of deity dwells in God!
He must be believed, and if you've believed in Jesus then you've believed in God!

That's my King!

He commands you to believe in Him, and the One Who commands you to believe in Him is God!
He must be honored just like His Father, and He Who must be honored just like the Father is God!
He gives eternal life to all those who have Him, and all those who have eternal life have God as their God!
In Him all things hold together, and all things hold together in God!
He tread upon the raging waves of the sea, and He who tread upon the raging waves of the sea is God!

CHRIST IS ALL!

He's the Holy, Holy, Holy One Whose glory fills the whole earth, and the Holy, Holy, Holy One Whose glory fills the whole earth is God!
He is called the everlasting Father, and the everlasting Father is God!
He possesses all authority in heaven and on earth, and all authority in heaven and on earth belongs to God!
If you know Him, then you know the Father, and if you know the Father, then you know God!
He possesses an everlasting dominion, and everlasting dominion belongs to God!

That's my King! Do you know Him?!

He healed by His Word, and He Who healed by His Word is God!
All things were created for Him and through Him, and all things created are from, through, and to God!
He alone can forgive sins, and He alone Who forgives sins is God!
We must all appear before His judgment seat, and He Whose judgment seat we must all appear before is God!
He judges everyone, and He Who judges everyone is God!
In Him, people are made new creations, and He Who makes all things new is God!
He's the One Creator, and the One Creator is God!
He's the Sower of the new covenant, and the Sower of the new covenant is God!

That's my King!

He's the King of kings, and the King of kings is God!
He reconciled the world to Himself, and He Who reconciled the world to Himself is God!
He's the King of Israel, and the King of Israel is God!
He's the Temple in heaven, and the Temple in heaven is God!
He's the One they looked on, on Him Whom they have pierced, and the One they looked on, on Him Whom they have pierced is God!

He must be everyone's only boast, and everyone's only boast must be in God!
HE'S THE ALL IN ALL, AND THE ALL IN ALL IS GOD!

That's my King! That's my King!

Here are numerous Scriptures confirming that Jesus Christ is the ALL IN ALL God-Man

1. Only God is my LORD and my God:
Psalm 35:23-24: my God and my Lord! Vindicate me, O LORD, my God
John 20:28: Thomas answered Him [Jesus], "My Lord and my God!"

2. Only God is the great I AM:
Exodus 3:14: God said to Moses, "I AM WHO I AM."
John 8:58: Jesus said to them, "Truly, truly, I say to you, before Abraham was, I AM."

3. Only God's blood was shed on the cross:
Acts 20:28: to care for the church of God, which He obtained with His own blood.
Ephesians 2:13: you who once were far off have been brought near by the blood of Christ.

4. Only God is the Husband:
Isaiah 54:5: For your Maker is your Husband, the LORD of hosts is His name
2 Corinthians 11:2: I betrothed you to one Husband, to present you as a pure virgin to Christ.

5. Only God gives life to the dead:
1 Samuel 2:6: The LORD kills and brings to life
John 5:21: so also the Son gives life to whom He will.

6. Only God is the Bridegroom:

Isaiah 62:5: For as a young man marries a young woman, so shall your sons marry you, and as the bridegroom rejoices over the bride, so shall your God rejoice over you.

Mark 2:19-20: And Jesus said to them, "Can the wedding guests fast while the bridegroom is with them? As long as they have the bridegroom with them, they cannot fast. The days will come when the bridegroom is taken away from them, and then they will fast in that day."

7. Only God is the Holy One:

Isaiah 43:15: I am the LORD, your Holy One, the Creator of Israel, your King.

Acts 3:14-15: But you denied the Holy and Righteous One, and asked for a murderer to be granted to you, and you killed the Author of life, Whom God raised from the dead. To this we are witnesses.

8. Only God is the I AM HE:

Isaiah 43:10: "You are My witnesses," declares the LORD, "and My servant whom I have chosen, that you may know and believe Me and understand that I am He. Before Me no god was formed, nor shall there be any after Me."

John 8:24: Jesus: "I told you that you would die in your sins, for unless you believe that I am He you will die in your sins."

9. Only God is the Alpha and the Omega:

Revelation 21:6: And He said to me, "It is done! I am the Alpha and the Omega, the Beginning and the End."

Revelation 22:13: Jesus: "I am the Alpha and the Omega"

10. Only God is the First and the Last:

Isaiah 44:6: Thus says the LORD . . . "I am the First and I am the Last"

Revelation 1:17-18: Jesus: "Fear not, I am the First and the Last, and the Living One. I died, and behold I am alive forevermore, and I have the keys of Death and Hades."

11. Only God is the Beginning and the End:
Revelation 21:6: And He said to me, "It is done! I am the Alpha and the Omega, the Beginning and the End."
Revelation 22:13: Jesus: "I am the Alpha and the Omega, the First and the Last, the Beginning and the End."

12. Only God is the One Master:
Jeremiah 3:14: Return, O faithless children, declares the LORD; for I am your Master
Luke 9:33: And as the men were parting from Him, Peter said to Jesus, "Master, it is good that we are here."

13. Only God is the Worthy One:
Revelation 4:11: Worthy are You, our Lord and God, to receive glory and honor and power, for You created all things, and by Your will they existed and were created.
Revelation 5:9: And they sang a new song, saying, "Worthy are You to take the scroll and to open its seals, for You were slain, and by Your blood You ransomed people for God from every tribe and language and people and nation"

14. Only God built all things:
Hebrews 3:4: (For every house is built by someone, but the builder of all things is God.)
Hebrews 3:3: For Jesus has been counted worthy of more glory than Moses – as much more glory as the builder of a house has more honor than the house itself.

15. Only God raised Jesus from the dead:
Romans 10:9: if you confess with your mouth that Jesus is Lord and believe in your heart that God raised Him from the dead, you will be saved.
John 2:19-21: Jesus answered them, "Destroy this temple, and in three days I will raise it up." The Jews then said, "It has taken forty-six years to build this temple, and will You raise it up in three days?" But He was speaking about the temple of His body.

16. Only God dwells in Christian believers:

2 Corinthians 6:16: What agreement has the temple of God with idols? For we are the temple of the living God; as God said, "I will make My dwelling among them and walk among them, and I will be their God, and they shall be My people."

Ephesians 3:17: so that Christ may dwell in your hearts through faith

Colossians 1:27: To them God chose to make known how great among the Gentiles are the riches of the glory of this mystery, which is Christ in you, the hope of glory.

17. Only God sanctifies Christian believers:

1 Thessalonians 5:23: Now may the God of peace Himself sanctify you completely

Ephesians 5:25-26: Husbands, love your wives, as Christ loved the church and gave Himself up for her, that He might sanctify her

18. Only God searches the heart of man:

Jeremiah 17:10: I the LORD search the heart and test the mind, to give every man according to his ways, according to the fruit of his deeds.

Revelation 2:23: Jesus: "And all the churches will know that I am He Who searches mind and heart, and I will give to each of you as your works deserve."

19. Only God reigns over Christian believers as slaves:

Romans 6:22: But now that you have been set free from sin and have become slaves of God, the fruit you get leads to sanctification and its end, eternal life.

1 Corinthians 7:22: For he who was called in the Lord as a slave is a freedman of the Lord. Likewise he who was free when called is a slave of Christ.

20. Only God is the Light:

Psalm 27:1: The LORD is my light

John 8:12: Jesus: "I am the light of the world."

21. Only God had a way prepared for Him:
Isaiah 40:3: A voice cries: "In the wilderness prepare the way of the LORD"
Mark 1:1-3: The beginning of the gospel of Jesus Christ, the Son of God. As it is written in Isaiah the prophet, "Behold, I send My messenger before your face, who will prepare your way, the voice of one crying in the wilderness: 'Prepare the way of the Lord, make His paths straight.'"

22. Only God is the same yesterday, today, and forever and does not change:
Malachi 3:6: For I the LORD do not change
Hebrews 13:8: Jesus Christ is the same yesterday and today and forever.

23. Only God is to be believed in for salvation:
John 12:44-45: And Jesus cried out and said, "Whoever believes in Me, believes not in Me but in Him Who sent Me. And whoever sees Me sees Him Who sent Me."
John 14:1: Jesus: "Let not your hearts be troubled. Believe in God; believe also in Me."

24. Only God can give eternal life:
1 John 5:11: And this is the testimony, that God gave us eternal life, and this life is in His Son.
John 10:27-28: Jesus: "My sheep hear My voice, and I know them, and they follow Me. I give them eternal life, and they will never perish, and no one will snatch them out of My hand."

25. Only God tread upon the raging waves:
Job 9:2, 8: Truly I know that it is so: But how can a man be in the right before God? . . . Who alone stretched out the heavens and trampled the waves of the sea
Matthew 14:24-25: but the boat by this time was a long way from the land, beaten by the waves, for the wind was against them. And in the fourth watch of the night He [Jesus] came to them, walking on the sea.

26. Only God is the Holy, Holy, Holy One Whose glory fills the whole earth:

Isaiah 6:1-3: In the year that King Uzziah died I saw the Lord sitting upon a throne, high and lifted up; and the train of His robe filled the temple. Above Him stood the seraphim. Each had six wings: with two he covered his face, and with two he covered his feet, and with two he flew. And one called to another and said: "Holy, Holy, Holy is the LORD of hosts; the whole earth is full of His glory!"

John 12:37-41: Though He [Jesus] had done so many signs before them, they still did not believe in Him, so that the word spoken by the prophet Isaiah might be fulfilled: "Lord, who has believed what he heard from us, and to whom has the arm of the Lord been revealed?" Therefore they could not believe. For again Isaiah said, "He has blinded their eyes and hardened their heart, lest they see with their eyes, and understand with their heart, and turn, and I would heal them." Isaiah said these things because he saw His [Jesus'] glory and spoke of Him [Jesus].

27. Only God possesses everlasting dominion:

Psalm 145:13: Your kingdom is an everlasting kingdom, and Your dominion endures throughout all generations. The LORD is faithful in all His words and kind in all His works.

Daniel 7:13-14: I saw in the night visions, and behold, with the clouds of heaven there came one like a son of man, and He came to the Ancient of Days and was presented before Him. And to Him was given dominion and glory and a kingdom, that all peoples, nations, and languages should serve Him; His dominion is an everlasting dominion, which shall not pass away, and His kingdom one that shall not be destroyed.

Mark 14:61-64: But He remained silent and made no answer. Again the high priest asked Him, "Are you the Christ, the Son of the Blessed?" And Jesus said, "I am, and you will see the Son of Man seated at the right hand of Power, and coming with the clouds of heaven." And the high priest tore his garments and said, "What further witnesses do we need? You have heard His blasphemy."

28. Only God can forgive sins:

Psalm 103:2-3: Bless the LORD . . . Who forgives all your iniquity

Luke 5:20-21: And when He [Jesus] saw their faith, He said, "Man, your sins are forgiven you." And the scribes and the Pharisees began to question, saying, "Who is this who speaks blasphemies? Who can forgive sins but God alone?"

29. Only God will judge everyone:

Acts 17:30-31: The times of ignorance God overlooked, but now He commands all people everywhere to repent, because He has fixed a day on which He will judge the world in righteousness by a Man Whom He has appointed; and of this He has given assurance to all by raising Him from the dead.

2 Timothy 4:1: I charge you in the presence of God and of Christ Jesus, Who is to judge the living and the dead

John 5:22: The Father judges no one, but has given all judgment to the Son

30. Only God is King of kings:

1 Timothy 6:13-16: I charge you in the presence of God, Who gives life to all things, and of Christ Jesus, Who in His testimony before Pontius Pilate made the good confession, to keep the commandment unstained and free from reproach until the appearing of our Lord Jesus Christ, which He will display at the proper time – He Who is the blessed and only Sovereign, the King of kings and Lord of lords, Who alone has immortality, Who dwells in unapproachable light, Whom no one has ever seen or can see. To Him be honor and eternal dominion. Amen.

Revelation 17:14: They will make war on the Lamb, and the Lamb will conquer them, for He is Lord of lords and King of kings, and those with Him are called and chosen and faithful.

31. Only God reconciled the world to Himself:

2 Corinthians 5:18-19: All this is from God, Who through Christ reconciled us to Himself and gave us the ministry of reconciliation; that is, in Christ God was reconciling the world to Himself, not counting their trespasses against them, and entrusting to us the message of reconciliation.

Colossians 1:19-20: For in Him [Jesus] all the fullness of God was pleased to dwell, and through Him to reconcile to Himself all things, whether on earth or in heaven, making peace by the blood of His cross.

32. Only God is the King of Israel:

Isaiah 44:6: Thus says the LORD, the King of Israel and his Redeemer, the LORD of hosts: "I am the First and I am the Last; besides Me there is no god."

John 1:49-50: Nathanael answered Him [Jesus], "Rabbi, You are the Son of God! You are the King of Israel!" Jesus answered him, "Because I said to you, 'I saw you under the fig tree,' do you believe? You will see greater things"

33. Only God is the Temple in heaven:

Revelation 21:22: And I saw no temple in the city, for its temple is the Lord God the Almighty and the Lamb.

34. Only God is to be prayed to:

Genesis 20:17: Then Abraham prayed to God

Acts 7:59: Stephen . . . called out, "Lord Jesus, receive my spirit."

35. Only God was pierced:

Zechariah 12:10: when they look on Me [the LORD], on Him Whom they have pierced

John 19:34: But one of the soldiers pierced His [Jesus'] side with a spear

36. Only God's Word stands forever:

Isaiah 40:8: the word of our God will stand forever

Luke 21:33: Jesus: "Heaven and earth will pass away, but My words will not pass away."

37. Only God is the Word:
John 1:1, 14: and the Word was God . . . And the Word became flesh and dwelt among us

38. Only God calmed the storming seas:
Psalm 65:5, 7: O God . . . Who stills the roaring of the seas
Mark 4:39: Jesus: "Peace! Be still!" And the wind ceased, and there was a great calm.

39. Only God is the Rock:
Deuteronomy 32:3-4: the LORD . . . The Rock
1 Corinthians 10:4: and the Rock was Christ.

40. Only God is the LORD of LORD's:
Deuteronomy 10:17: For the LORD your God is God of gods and Lord of lords
Revelation 19:16: On His [Jesus'] robe and on His thigh He has a name written, King of kings and Lord of lords.

41. Only God's name is God:
Matthew 1:23: they shall call His [Jesus'] name Immanuel (which means, God with us).

42. Only God is the Shepherd:
Psalm 23:1: The LORD is my shepherd
John 10:11: Jesus: "I am the good shepherd."

43. Only God's name can save:
Psalm 54:1: O God, save me, by Your name, and vindicate me by Your might.
Acts 4:12: And there is salvation in no one else, for there is no other name [Jesus] under heaven given among men by which we must be saved.

44. Only God is the Savior:
Isaiah 43:3: For I am the LORD your God, the Holy One of Israel, your Savior.
Luke 2:11: For unto you is born this day in the city of David a Savior, Who is Christ the Lord.

45. Only God is the Redeemer:
Isaiah 41:14: the LORD; your Redeemer is the Holy One of Israel.
Galatians 3:13: Christ redeemed us from the curse of the law by becoming a curse for us

46. Only God is worthy to receive glory, honor, and power:
Revelation 4:11: Worthy are You, our Lord and God, to receive glory and honor and power
Revelation 5:13: To Him Who sits on the throne and to the Lamb [Jesus] be blessing and honor and glory and might forever and ever!

47. Only God is equal with the Father:
James 3:9: we bless our Lord and Father
John 10:30: Jesus: "I and the Father are one."
John 14:7: Jesus: "If you had known Me, you would have known my Father also. From now on you do know Him and have seen Him."
John 14:9, 11: Jesus: "Whoever has seen Me has seen the Father . . . Believe Me that I am in the Father and the Father is in Me"
John 5:18: He was even calling God His own Father, making Himself equal with God.
John 5:22-23: Jesus: "The Father judges no one, but has given all judgment to the Son, that all may honor the Son, just as they honor the Father."

48. Only God must be worshiped:
Revelation 19:10: You must not do that! . . . Worship God.
Hebrews 1:6: Let all God's angels worship Him [Jesus].

49. Only God is the Wonderful Counselor:
Isaiah 28:29: This also comes from the LORD of hosts; He is wonderful in counsel and excellent in wisdom.
Isaiah 9:6: For to us a Child is born, to us a Son is given . . . His [Jesus'] name shall be called Wonderful Counselor

50. Only God is the Mighty God:
Jeremiah 32:18: O great and mighty God, Whose name is the LORD of hosts
Isaiah 9:6: For to us a Child is born, to us a Son is given . . . His [Jesus'] name shall be called . . . Mighty God

51. Only God is the Everlasting Father:
Psalm 90:2: from everlasting to everlasting you are God.
Isaiah 9:6: For to us a Child is born, to us a Son is given . . . His [Jesus'] name shall be called . . . Everlasting Father

52. Only God's throne is forever and ever:
Lamentations 5:19: But You, O LORD, reign forever; Your throne endures to all generations.
Hebrews 1:8: But of the Son He says, "Your throne, O God, is forever and ever."

53. Only God is God over all:
Ephesians 4:6: God and Father Who is over all
Romans 9:5: the Christ Who is God over all

54. Only God is omnipresent:
Jeremiah 23:24: "Can a man hide himself in secret places so that I cannot see him? . . . Do I not fill heaven and earth?" declares the Lord.
Matthew 18:20: Jesus: "For where two or three are gathered in My name, there am I among them."

55. Only God is the Great and True God:
Psalm 95:3: For the LORD is a great God
Titus 2:13: our great God and Savior Jesus Christ
1 John 5:20: His Son Jesus Christ. He is the true God
2 Peter 1:1: our God and Savior Jesus Christ

56. Only God is the LORD our righteousness:
Jeremiah 23:6: And this is the name by which He will be called: "The LORD is our righteousness."
1 Corinthians 1:30: Christ Jesus, Whom God made our wisdom and our righteousness

57. Only God created all things:
Genesis 1:1: In the beginning, God created the heavens and the earth.
John 1:3: All things were made through Him [Jesus], and without Him was not any thing made that was made.

58. Only calling on God can save you:
Joel 2:32: everyone who calls on the name of the LORD shall be saved.
Romans 10:10-13: For with the heart one believes and is justified, and with the mouth one confesses and is saved. For the Scripture says, "Everyone who believes in Him will not be put to shame." For there is no distinction between Jew and Greek; the same Lord is Lord of all, bestowing His riches on all who call on Him. For "everyone who calls on the name of the Lord will be saved."

59. Only to God must every knee bow:
Isaiah 45:22-23: For I am God, and there is no other . . . To Me every knee shall bow, every tongue shall swear allegiance.
Philippians 2:10-11: so that at the name of Jesus every knee should bow . . . and every tongue confess that Jesus Christ is Lord

60. Only God is the fulness of deity:
Deuteronomy 7:9: Know therefore that the LORD your God is God
Colossians 2:9: For in Christ all the fullness of the Deity lives in bodily form

61. Only in God do all things hold together:
Nehemiah 9:6: You are the LORD, You alone. You have made heaven, the heaven of heavens, with all their host, the earth and all that is on it, the seas and all that is in them; and You preserve all of them
Colossians 1:17: And He [Jesus] is before all things, and in Him all things hold together.

62. Only at God's judgment seat will all be judged:
Romans 14:10: For we will all stand before the judgment seat of God
2 Corinthians 5:10: For we must all appear before the judgment seat of Christ

63. Only God is to be boasted in:
Jeremiah 9:24: let him who boasts boast in this, that he understands and knows Me, that I am the LORD
Philippians 3:3: boast in Christ Jesus

64. You can only have God the Father if you have God the Son also:
1 John 2:22-23: Who is the liar but he who denies that Jesus is the Christ? This is the antichrist, he who denies the Father and the Son. No one who denies the Son has the Father. Whoever confesses the Son has the Father also.

65. Only God is to be trusted in:
Jeremiah 17:5, 7: Thus says the LORD: "Cursed is the man who trusts in man and makes flesh his strength, whose heart turns away from the LORD . . . Blessed is the man who trusts in the LORD, whose trust is the LORD."
1 Thessalonians 1:3: and labor of love and steadfastness of trust in our Lord Jesus Christ.
1 Timothy 1:1: and of Christ Jesus our trust

66. Only God is the ALL in ALL:
1 Corinthians 15:28: that God may be all in all!
Colossians 3:11: but Christ is all, and in all!

JESUS CHRIST IS GOD!

Unless you honor the Son just as you honor the Father (John 5:23) and, like Thomas (see #1), call Him "My LORD and my God!" – you cannot be saved.

Please trust in God the Son today!

Precious Jesus! All in all to me Thou art!

Octavius Winslow

O Jesus, nothing may I see,
Nothing desire, or seek, but Thee.

Paul Gerhardt

. . . when the Scripture sets Jesus Christ before us, it is not
without cause that we are told to rest wholly upon Him,
and keep to Him when we have come to Him, because He
has all fulness of good things in Himself. Therefore we do
not need to be wandering here and there, or taking such
great trouble in seeking the things that are needful for us.
In short, we must no longer go astray, but must adhere
wholly to Him, as to our perfect and sovereign happiness.

John Calvin

4
"THAT'S MY KING!"
WHO HAS THE NAME
ABOVE ALL NAMES!

He's Jesus Christ the Righteous!
He's Savior!
He's Immanuel!
He's Teacher!
He's Rabboni!
He's Master!
He's Governor!
He's Law Giver!
He's Forerunner!
He's Redeemer!
He's Messiah!
He's Shiloh!
He's Deliverer!
He's Mediator!
He's Intercessor!
He's Prince!
He's Mighty to Save!

Now that's my King!

CHRIST IS ALL!

He's The Surety of a Better Testament!
He's The Just One!
He's The Holy One!
He's The Holy and The Just!
He's The Holy and Righteous One!
He's The Holy One of God!
He's The Faithful and True Witness!
He's The Witness to the People!
He's The Leader and Commander of the People!
He's The Consolation of Israel!
He's The Lion of the Tribe of Judah!

That's my King! I wonder if you know Him today?!

He's Jesus!
He's The Young Child!
He's The Holy Child!
He's The Nazarene!
He's Jesus of Nazareth!
He's Lord!
He's The Lord from Heaven!
He's The Lord of Glory!
He's The LORD Our Righteousness!
He's The Lord of the Holy Prophets!
He's Lord and Savior!
He's My Lord and My God!
He's The Holy One of God!

That's my King!

He's The First Fruits!
He's The First Begotten!
He's The Elect of God!
He's The Branch of Righteousness!
He's The Second Adam!
He's The Last Adam!
He's The King of Zion!
He's The King of the Jews!
He's The King of Israel!

CHRIST IS ALL!

He's The King of the Saints!
He's The Prince of the Kings of the Earth!
He's The King Eternal, Immortal, Invisible, God Manifest
in the Flesh!

That's my King! Do you know Him?!

He's The Righteous Judge!
He's The Judge of Israel!
He's The Judge of All the Earth!
He's The Desire of All the Nations!
He's The Signal of the People!
He's The Captain of the Lord's Army!
He's The Banner upon the High Mountain!

That's my King!

He's The Messenger of the High Covenant!
He's The Minister of the Sanctuary!
He's The Author and the Finisher of Our Faith!
He's our Advocate!
He's our Peace!
He's our Ransom!
He's our Passover!
He's our Great High Priest!
He's The High Priest Forever after the order of
Melchizedek!
He's The King of Righteousness!
He's The King of Peace!
He's The King of Kings, and He's The Lord of Lords!

Now that's my King!

He's Jesus Christ!
He's Lord and Christ!
He's The Lord's Christ!
He's The Christ of God!
He's The Lord Jesus Christ!
He's Lord of Sabaoth!
He's Lord of Hosts!

CHRIST IS ALL!

He's Lord of the Sabbath!
He's Lord of Heaven and Earth!
He's Jesus Christ our Lord!
He's our Lord and Savior Jesus Christ!
He's The Savior of the World!

That's my King!

He's The Man Christ Jesus!
He's a Man Approved of God!
He's our Elder Brother!
He's The First Born among many brothers!
He's a Friend Who sticks closer than a brother!
He's The Master!
He's your Master!
He's your Lord and Master!
He's The Good Master!

That's my King!

He's The Horn of Salvation!
He's The Captain of Our Salvation!
He's The Brightness of the Father's Glory!
He's The Glory as of the Only Begotten!
He's The Image of the Invisible God!
He's The Express Image of His Person!
He's The Fullness of Deity Bodily!
He's The Bridegroom!
He's The Beginning of the Creation of God!

That's my King! I wonder if you know Him today?!

He's The Way!
He's The Truth!
He's The Life!
He's The Tree of Life!
He's The Light of Life!
He's The Word of Life!
He's The Bread of Life!

CHRIST IS ALL!

He's The Prince of Life!
He's Life Eternal!
He's The Water of Life!
He's The Living Water!
He's The Living Bread!
He's The Bread which came down from Heaven!
He's The True Bread from Heaven!
He's The Hidden Manna!

That's my King!

He's The Door!
He's The Door of the Sheep!
He's The Chief Shepherd!
He's The Good Shepherd!
He's The Shepherd and Bishop of your souls!
He's The Lamb without Spot or Blemish!
He's The Lamb Who was Slain!
He's The Vine!
He's The True Vine!
He's The Root of Jesse!
He's The Root and Offspring of David!
He's The Prophet of Nazareth!
He's a Prophet mighty in word and deed!
He's The Prophet of the Highest!

That's my King!

He's The Morning Star!
He's The Day Spring from on High!
He's The Heir of All Things!
He's The Tried Stone!
He's The Living Stone!
He's The Sure Foundation!
He's The Stone Chosen of God and precious!
He's The Spiritual Rock!
He's The Rock of Ages!
He's The Faithful and True Witness!
He's The Apostle and High Priest of our Profession!

CHRIST IS ALL!

He's The Great I AM!

That's my King! Do you know Him?!

He's The Man of Sorrows!
He's The Friend of tax collectors and sinners!
He's The Gift of God!
He's The Unspeakable Gift!
He's God Blessed Forever!
He's The Light of the world!
He's The Quickening Spirit!
He's The First Fruits of them that sleep!
He's The First Begotten of the Dead!
He's The Resurrection and the Life!

That's my King!

He's The Chief Cornerstone!
He's The Head of the Church!
He's The Head of Every Man!
He's The True Light Who enlightens everyone Who has
come into the world!
He's The Rose of Sharon!
He's The Lily of the Valley!
He's The Altogether Lovely One!
He's The Fairest among Ten Thousand!
He's The Bright and Morning Star!
He's The Power of God!
He's The Wisdom of God!
He's The Word of God!
He's The Image of God!
He's The Lamb of God Who takes away the sin of the
world!
He's God's Elect!

That's my King!

He's The First and the Last!
He's The Beginning and the End!
He's The Alpha and The Omega!

CHRIST IS ALL!

He's The Ancient of Days!
He's The Blessed and Only Potentate!
He's God with Us!
He's God Our Savior!
He's The Only Wise God Our Savior!
He's The Lord Who Is, Who Was, and Who Is to Come!
He's The Almighty!
He's Wonderful!
He's The Counselor!
He's The Mighty God!
He's The Everlasting Father!
He's The Prince of Peace!
He's The Branch!

That's my King! Do you know Him?!

He's The Son of Mary!
He's The Son of Man!
He's The Son of David!
He's The Son of Abraham!
He's The Son of the Blessed!
He's The Sun of Righteousness!
He's The Son of the Highest!
He's The Son of God!
He's The Son of the Living God!
He's God's Dear Son!
He's The Son of His Love!
He's The Only Begotten Son of God!
He's God's Beloved Son in Whom He was, is, and
forevermore will be well pleased!
He has The Name that Is Above Every Name!

That's my King! That's my King!

Clinton N. Howard compiled these (more than 200) names
of our Lord Jesus after he was challenged by a Muslim
nobleman whose rosary included 99 names for Allah. Mr.
Howard published these names in 1925 under the title
"Pearls of Paradise," at the request of William Jennings
Bryan.

41

Though all the world my choice deride,
Yet Jesus shall my portion be;
For I am pleased with none beside;
The fairest of the fair is He.

Gerhard Tersteegen

Object of my first desire,
Jesus crucified for me;
All to happiness aspire,
Only to be found in Thee.
Let me but Thyself possess,
Total sum of happiness:
Perfect peace I then shall prove,
Heaven below and heaven above.

Augustus Toplady

Have ye renounced all other things for your all,
and have ye received Him to be your all?

Philip Henry

5
"THAT'S MY KING!"
WHO GRANTS YOU
YOUR TRUE IDENTITY!

By grace through faith in my King Jesus . . .

You're justified and have peace with God!

You died with Christ and died to the power of sin's rule over your life!

Your enemies should not rejoice over you for when you fall, you will arise; when you sit in darkness, the LORD will be a light to you. You will bear the indignation of the LORD because you have sinned against Him, until He pleads your case and executes justice for you. He will bring you forth to the light; You will see His righteousness!

That's my King!

Your God is unlike any other, pardoning iniquity and passing over the transgression of the remnant of His heritage. He does not retain His anger forever, because He delights in mercy.

CHRIST IS ALL!

He will again have compassion on you, and will subdue your iniquities. He will cast all your sins into the depths of the sea!

Your sins have been removed from you as far as the east is from the west!

Your sins have all been cast behind the LORD's back!

Your sins have been blotted out for His own sake, and He will remember them no more!

That's my King!

Though your sins are like scarlet, they shall be as white as snow!

Jesus was wounded for your transgressions; bruised for your iniquities; and the chastisement for your peace was upon Him!

You're free from condemnation forever!

Where your sin abounds, grace abounds for you all the more!

Your God is gracious and merciful, slow to anger and abounding in steadfast love, One who relents from doing harm!

You're kept as the apple of God's eye!

That's who you are in my King! I wonder if you know Him today?!

Your God has no pleasure in the death of the wicked, but that the wicked turn from his ways and live!

If you come to Jesus, He will by no means cast you out!

CHRIST IS ALL!

You'll not perish, but you'll have everlasting life!

You've been saved from the fierceness of God's everlasting wrath in hell where the fire is unquenchable and where there will be weeping and gnashing of teeth!

You have Christ as your wisdom, righteousness, sanctification, and redemption and have been made righteous!

You have the mind of Christ!

You're the temple of the Holy Spirit, were bought with a price, and are not your own!

You've been established in Christ, sealed, and you have been given the Spirit in your heart as a guarantee of your inheritance!

You've been crucified with Christ; it is no longer you who live, but Christ lives in you!

That's my King!

You've been blessed with every spiritual blessing in the heavenly places in Christ!

You've been chosen in Christ before the foundation of the world, that you should be holy and without blame before Him in love!

You've been predestined to adoption as sons of God!

You've been made alive together with Christ!

You've been made to sit together in the heavenly places in Christ Jesus!

You have access by one Spirit to the Father!

CHRIST IS ALL!

You have boldness and access to God with confidence through faith in Him!

You've been delivered from the power of darkness and conveyed into the kingdom of the Son of His love, in Whom we have redemption through His blood, the forgiveness of sins!

Christ is in you!

That's your blessed identity in my King!

You're complete in Christ!

You've not been given a spirit of fear, but of power and of love and of a sound mind!

You're sanctified and one with the Sanctifier, therefore Jesus calls you His brother!

You can come boldly to the throne of grace, that you may obtain mercy and find grace to help in time of need!

You've been given exceedingly great and precious promises, that through them you may be partakers of the divine nature!

You're the salt of the earth and the light of the world!

Jesus calls you His friend!

You were chosen by Jesus and appointed by Him to go and bear lasting fruit!

You're a slave of righteousness and a slave of God!

You're an heir of God and a joint heir with Christ!

That's my King!

CHRIST IS ALL!

You're a member of the body of Christ!

You're a new creation!

You're a saint!

You're holy and righteous!

Your life is hidden with Christ in God!

You're the elect of God, holy and beloved!

You're a chosen generation, a royal priesthood, a holy nation, His own special people, the people of God!

You can do all things through Christ Who strengthens you!

You have all your needs supplied according to God's riches in glory by Christ Jesus!

You have the LORD as the strength of your life and as your confidence!

That's the truth about you as a son or daughter of the King!

Are you content in Him alone today?!

You shall always be led by God to triumph in Christ!

You can cast all your worries, fears, and anxieties on God because He cares for you!

You're never alone for Christ is always with you!

You should boast in your weaknesses that the power of Christ may rest upon you because His grace is sufficient for you, for His strength is made perfect in weakness!

CHRIST IS ALL!

You're not a lot of things you should be, but take heart: God has chosen the things which are not, to bring to nothing the things that are that no flesh should glory in His presence!

You have your sufficiency from God!

You have God working in you both to will and to do for His good pleasure!

You'll do valiantly through God, for it is He Who shall tread down your enemies!

That's my King!

You'll have fullness of joy and pleasures forevermore one day forever in God's very presence!

Your momentary and light affliction, which is for a moment, is working for you a far more exceeding and eternal weight of glory!

Your present sufferings are not worthy to be compared with the glory which shall be revealed in you!

One day you shall have no more tears, no more sorrow, no more pain; there shall be no more death and no more sin!

You shall not be separated from the love of Christ for any reason in the universe!

You have certain and unshakable promises causing you to be strong, courageous, and fearless because God is with you, and He is your God and will strengthen you and help you and uphold you with His righteous right hand!

You'll one day enter into the joy of your LORD!

That's what you'll get in my King!

CHRIST IS ALL!

Your hairs are numbered and if not even a little bird can fall to the ground apart from God's will, you should fear nothing, for God loves you much more than little birds!

In His book they all were written – every detail of every day fashioned by Him for your good before even one came into being!

All your times are in His hands!

As your days are, so shall your strength be and underneath are the everlasting arms!

All things work according to His will!

If you sin, you have an advocate with the Father, Jesus Christ the righteous!

That's my King!

If you confess your sins, He is faithful and just to forgive you your sins and to cleanse you from all unrighteousness!

You can never be defeated because if God is for you, who can be against you?!

You're more than a conqueror through Him who loved you!

All things, even those things meant for evil against you, are working for your good!

You are loved by God with an everlasting love!

Your right hand is held by God, and He will guide you with His counsel!

God satisfies you with the fullness of His house and gives you drink from the river of His pleasures!

God delights in you, and as a bridegroom rejoices over his bride, so shall your God rejoice over you!

God, the Mighty Warrior, is with you, and He will rejoice over you with gladness; He will calm all your fears with His love; and He will rejoice over you with loud songs!

You are God's special treasure!

Your heavenly Father, like the Hound of Heaven, is pursuing you relentlessly with goodness and mercy all the days of your life, and you shall dwell in His house forever!

That's your identity in your King!

That's my King! That's my King!

Fighting To Delight In Your King Through Suffering

The way to be more than a conqueror over every fear, every painful loss, every unfulfilled desire, every disappointment, every tough situation, every divorce, every broken relationship, every hope deferred, and every other painful loss is to fix your eyes on Jesus, the Author and Finisher of your faith.

Forget about yourself and your circumstances and thank Jesus, praise Jesus, and boast in Jesus alone. Meditate on Him, His perfect work, and Who you are in Him. Having Jesus Christ as your all in all and Christ in you the hope of glory is the answer to every hope and dream deferred. For He must be our greatest hope and dream Who will never leave us nor forsake us. If you are in Christ Jesus by grace through faith, the following truths are true of you, and they will be precious to you.

CHRIST IS ALL!

For to those who believe He is precious . . .

On the cross, the peace Jesus formerly enjoyed with His Father was turned into anger, suffering, and pain as He suffered the wrath of the Father that you deserved because of your sin. Because of Jesus' sufferings, you are justified and have peace with God. Romans 5:1

On the cross, Jesus endured the condemnation you deserved, so that now you are free from condemnation forever. Romans 8:1

On the cross, Jesus was crushed for all your sins – past, present, and future – so that now where your sin abounds, grace abounds for you all the more. Romans 5:20

In Jesus are all the treasures of wisdom and knowledge. He is the perfectly righteous One and the perfectly sanctified One. And now you have Him as your wisdom, righteousness, sanctification, and redemption.
1 Corinthians 1:30

Jesus was made your sin and crushed on the cross, so that now you are made righteous in Him.
2 Corinthians 5:21

Jesus is the Lion of the tribe of Judah and the Lamb Who was slain, so that now you are righteous and bold as a lion. Proverbs 28:1

Your sins were brought near to Jesus, counted as His, and He suffered for them, so that now they are removed from you as far as the east is from the west. Psalm 103:12

Your sins were met head on by the Father as He punished them in Jesus on the cross, so that now they have all been cast behind the LORD's back. Isaiah 38:17

CHRIST IS ALL!

The Father remembered your sins in Jesus on the cross, so that now they have been blotted out for His own sake, and He will remember them no more. Isaiah 43:25

Jesus, Who is as clean as the purest white, was made filthy with your sins, so that now, though your sins are like scarlet, they shall be as white as snow. Isaiah 1:18

Jesus conquered every temptation He ever faced and never sinned once in the smallest way. He was obedient all the way unto death on the cross, so that now, by grace through faith, you died with Him and died to the power of sin's rule over your life. Romans 6:1-6

Jesus was wounded for your transgressions; bruised for your iniquities; and the chastisement for your peace was upon Him. Isaiah 53:5

Jesus was made and treated like an enemy of God and utterly vanquished on the cross, so that now your enemies should not rejoice over you. For when you fall, you shall arise; when you sit in darkness, the LORD shall be a light to you. You shall bear the indignation of the LORD because you have sinned against Him, until He pleads your case and executes justice for you. He will bring you forth to the light; You will see His righteousness. Micah 7:8-9

God did not merely pardon your sins or pass over your transgressions. Instead, He chose not to restrain His anger or have mercy on His own Son, but He delighted to crush Jesus on the cross in your place. Therefore, your God is unlike any other, pardoning iniquity and passing over the transgression of the remnant of His heritage. He does not retain His anger forever, because He delights in mercy. He will again have compassion on you, and will subdue your iniquities. He will cast all your sins into the depths of the sea. Micah 7:18-19

On the cross where His Son hung, the Father showed no grace or mercy; displayed the full measure of His anger; hid His lovingkindness; and did not relent from doing harm to His own Son, so that now He might be gracious and merciful to you; slow to anger and abundant in lovingkindness; One who relents from doing harm against you because Jesus paid it all. Jonah 4:2

Jesus, Who alone earned the right to have the highest honor in the Father's eyes, was abandoned on that cross, so that now you might be kept as the apple of God's eye. Deuteronomy 32:10

Jesus died in the place of the wicked Barabbas and in the place of all those wicked ones His Father had given Him because the Father has no pleasure in the death of the wicked, but that the wicked turn from his way and live. Ezekiel 33:11

On the cross, Jesus was cast out and forsaken by the Father, so that now if you come to Jesus, He will by no means cast you out. John 6:37

On the cross, Jesus perished in your place, so that now if you believe in Him, you will not perish, but you will have everlasting life. John 3:16

Jesus faced the fierceness of God's infinite wrath on the cross, so that now you have been saved from this infinite, everlasting wrath in hell where the fire is unquenchable and where there will be weeping and gnashing of teeth. Mark 9:43; Matthew 8:12; 25:46

Jesus has the greatest mind in the universe. No one can instruct Him! His mind is the most wise, the most knowledgeable, the most keen, the most humble. And in Him, you have the mind of Christ. 1 Corinthians 2:16

CHRIST IS ALL!

Jesus is the Temple Who was torn down and rebuilt in three days. He is the most beautiful, the most glorious, the most precious Temple of the LORD. And by grace through faith, you are united to Him. You are the temple of the Holy Spirit; you were bought with a price; and you are not your own, for Jesus purchased you with His own blood.
1 Corinthians 6:19-20

Jesus was established as no other, and He had the Holy Spirit upon Him in power. And you have been established in Christ, sealed, and you have been given the Holy Spirit in your heart as a guarantee of your inheritance.
2 Corinthians 1:21; Ephesians 1:13-14

Jesus was crucified but rose again in power and glory to newness of life, conquering sin, death, and Satan. And you have been crucified with Christ; it is no longer you who live, but Christ lives in you. Galatians 2:20

Jesus embodied and lived out every spiritual blessing imaginable, and you have been blessed with every spiritual blessing in the heavenly places in Christ. Ephesians 1:3

Jesus is the holiest of the holy and the most blameless of the blameless. And you have been chosen in Christ before the foundation of the world, that you should be holy and without blame before Him in love. Ephesians 1:4

Jesus is the preeminent Son of God. And you have been predestined to adoption as sons of God. Ephesians 1:5;
1 John 3:1

Though He died on the cross, Jesus is alive! You too have been made alive together with Christ. Ephesians 2:5

Jesus came down from the heavenly places to be mocked, mistreated, beaten, and killed because of your sin, so that now you have been made to sit together in the heavenly places in Christ Jesus. Ephesians 2:6

Jesus' access to the Father was cut off on the cross, so that now you have access by one Spirit to the Father. Ephesians 2:18

You have boldness and access to God with confidence through faith in Him. Ephesians 3:12

Darkness overcame Jesus on the cross, so that now you have been delivered from the power of darkness and conveyed into the kingdom of the Son of His love, in Whom we have redemption through His blood, the forgiveness of sins. Colossians 1:13-14

Jesus suffered for you, so that now Christ is in you. Colossians 1:27

Jesus lacked everything on the cross, so that now you are complete in Christ. Colossians 2:10

In the Garden of Gethsemane, Jesus deeply feared the wrath of God, and He feared being excluded from the presence of His Father, so that now you have not been given a spirit of fear, but of power and of love and of a sound mind. 2 Timothy 1:7

Jesus is the perfectly sanctified One. In Him, you are sanctified and one with the Sanctifier, therefore Jesus calls you His brother. Hebrews 2:11

On the cross, Jesus was cut off from God's grace, obtained no mercy, and found no help from anyone in His greatest time of need, so that now you can come boldly to the throne of grace, that you may obtain mercy and find grace to help in time of need. Hebrews 4:16

All the fullness of the Godhead dwells in Jesus bodily, and through His perfect work you have been given exceedingly great and precious promises, that through them you may be partakers of the divine nature. 2 Peter 1:4

CHRIST IS ALL!

Jesus is the saltiest Salt and the brightest Light of the world, so that now, in Him, you are the salt of the earth and the light of the world. Matthew 5:13-14

Jesus is a friend of tax collectors and sinners, and now He calls you His friend. John 15:15

Jesus produced the most beautiful, sweetest, and longest lasting fruit through His life and death, so that now you are chosen and appointed by Him to go and bear lasting fruit. John 15:16

Jesus was the most submissive, joyful, righteous, and obedient slave of God ever to live on earth, so that now you are a slave of righteousness and a slave of God. Romans 6:18, 22

Jesus left all His glorious, heavenly inheritance to come to earth, take on human flesh, and suffer for your sins. In Him, you are an heir of God and a joint heir with Christ. Romans 8:17

Jesus gave His body to be beaten, hit, spit upon, and crucified, so that now you are a member of the body of Christ. Ephesians 5:30

Through Jesus' death and resurrection, the first fruits of the new creation have arrived, so that now, in Christ, you are a new creation. 2 Corinthians 5:17

Jesus was the greatest Saint to ever live, so that now, in Him, you also are a saint. Ephesians 1:1

Jesus was holy and righteous like no other, so that now, in Him, you are holy and righteous too. Ephesians 4:24

Jesus was exposed, naked, and abandoned on the cross, so that now your life is hidden with Christ in God. Colossians 3:4

Jesus, the beloved Son in Whom the Father is well pleased, was made an object of wrath on the cross, so that now you are the elect of God, holy and beloved. Colossians 3:12

Jesus, the only true Person of God Who alone lived a fully pleasing life in the Father's sight, was the Priest Who interceded with His own body on the cross, so that now you are a chosen generation, a royal priesthood, a holy nation, His own special people, the people of God. 1 Peter 2:9-10

On the cross, all Jesus' strength was dried up. He was a man Who had no strength, so that now you can do all things through Christ Who strengthens you.
Philippians 4:13

On the cross, Jesus did not even receive a cup of water when He needed it, so that now you have all your needs supplied according to God's riches in glory in Christ Jesus.
Philippians 4:19

On the cross, Jesus seemed to lose all confidence when He cried out, "My God, My God, why have You forsaken Me?!" so that now you have the LORD as the strength of your life and as your confidence. Psalm 27:1; Proverbs 3:26

In His glorious death and resurrection, Jesus triumphed over all His and your enemies, so that now you shall always be led by God to triumph in Christ. 2 Corinthians 2:14

In the Garden of Gethsemane and on the cross, Jesus endured and triumphed over the greatest worries, fears, and anxieties ever known to man, so that now you can cast all your worries, fears, and anxieties on God because He cares for you. 1 Peter 5:7

On the cross, Jesus was forsaken and left utterly alone, so that now you are never alone, for Christ is always with you, and He will never leave you nor forsake you.
Matthew 28:20; Hebrews 13:5

CHRIST IS ALL!

On the cross, Jesus manifested the ultimate picture of the greatest strength in the most lowly weakness, so that now you should boast in your weaknesses that the power of Christ may rest upon you because His grace is sufficient for you, for His strength is made perfect in weakness.
2 Corinthians 12:9

Through the cross of Christ, God brought the greatest good out of the greatest evil, so that now, though you are not a lot of things you should be, you can take heart since God has chosen the things which are not, to bring to nothing the things that are, so that no flesh should glory in His presence. 1 Corinthians 1:28-29

Through the resurrection of Jesus, God did what is impossible for man. Therefore, your God is the God of the impossible, so that now in any and every painful, hopeless situation, against hope you can hope in your great God of the impossible! Your God is the God of the resurrection so you can grow strong in your faith, giving glory to God!
Romans 4:16-21

Through the cross, Jesus purchased all you need for life, ministry, and godliness, so that now you have all you need – your sufficiency is from God, and He is able to make all grace abound to you, so that having all sufficiency in all things at all times, you may abound in every good work.
2 Corinthians 3:5, 9:8

On the cross, Jesus was a fragrant offering and a well pleasing sacrifice to God, so that now you have God working in you both to will and to do for His good pleasure.
Ephesians 5:2; Philippians 2:13

On the cross, Jesus more than conquered all your enemies, so that now you will do valiantly through God, for it is He Who shall tread down your enemies. Psalm 60:12

CHRIST IS ALL!

On the cross, Jesus was shut out of the glorious, all satisfying presence of His Father because of your sin, so that now you will have fullness of joy and pleasures forever more one day forever in God's very presence. Psalm 16:11

On the cross, Jesus endured the weightiest and most infinite affliction in your place, so that now your momentary and light affliction, which is for a moment, is working for you a far more exceeding and eternal weight of glory, and your present sufferings are not worthy to be compared with the glory which shall be revealed in you. 2 Corinthians 4:17; Romans 8:18

In His life and death, Jesus shed many tears and endured much pain and sorrow on your behalf, so that now you have certainty that one day you shall have no more tears, no more sorrow, no more pain; there shall be no more death and no more sin. Revelation 21:4

The Father's love for the Son is infinitely great. Yet He did not spare His own Son but delivered Him up for us all. Therefore, since He has given us the greatest gift imaginable in His Son, surely He will also freely give us all things. Romans 8:32

In His life and death, Jesus experienced tribulation, distress, persecution, hunger, thirst, nakedness, peril, and the nails and spear at the cross, so that now you shall not be separated from the love of Christ for any of these reasons or for any other reason in the universe. No trial in your life should ever make you doubt God's love for you. Even in all your hardships, God's love is strong toward you. He has given the greatest evidence of His love for you at the cross. Romans 8:35-39

On the cross, the Father did not come to Jesus' aid, so that now you have certain and unshakable promises causing you to be strong, courageous, and fearless because God is with you, and He is your God and will strengthen you and help you and uphold you with His righteous right hand. Isaiah 41:10

On the cross, Jesus was excluded from the joy of the LORD, so that now you will one day enter into the joy of your LORD. Matthew 25:23

Jesus went to the cross according to the definite plan and foreknowledge of God, and His enemies were gathered against Him to do whatever God's hand and His purpose determined before to be done. Therefore, since God is in absolute control of the most wicked action in the universe (the crucifixion of Jesus), and He worked it for your good, you can rest assured in the following truths about God's absolute sovereignty working for your good.
Acts 2:22-23, 4:27-28

Your hairs are all numbered, and if not even a little bird can fall to the ground apart from God's will, you should fear nothing, for God loves you much more than little birds. Matthew 10:29-31

In His book they all were written – every detail of every day fashioned by Him for your good before even one came into being. Psalm 139:16

All your times are in His hands. Psalm 31:15

All things work according to His will. Ephesians 1:11

As your days are, so shall your strength be, and underneath are the everlasting arms. Deuteronomy 33:25; 27

Your right hand is held by God, and He will guide you with His counsel. Psalm 73:23-24

All things, even those things meant for evil against you, are working for your good. Romans 8:28

Because of Jesus' perfect life and death, if you sin, you have an advocate with the Father, Jesus Christ the righteous. 1 John 2:1

If you confess your sins, He is faithful and just to forgive you your sins and to cleanse you from all unrighteousness. 1 John 1:9

On the cross, the Father was against Jesus, condemning Him for your sake, so that now you can never be condemned because God is absolutely for you forever. Romans 8:31

In His death and resurrection, Jesus conquered all powers, enemies, and evils, so that now you are more than a conqueror through Him Who loved you. Romans 8:37

On the cross, Jesus was crushed by God with the equivalent of myriads of everlasting punishments in hell, so that now you are reconciled to God because you've been loved with an everlasting love. Jeremiah 31:3

On the cross, Jesus was cut off from the fullness of God's house and from drinking from the river of His pleasures, so that now God satisfies you with the fullness of His house and gives you drink from the river of His pleasures. Psalm 36:8

On the cross, the Father delighted to bruise the Son, so that now God delights in you, and as a bridegroom rejoices over his bride, so shall your God rejoice over you. Isaiah 62:4-5

On the cross, the Father punished His only beloved Son, so that now God, the Mighty Warrior, is with you, and He will rejoice over you with gladness, He will calm all your fears with His love, and He will rejoice over you with loud songs! Zephaniah 3:17

CHRIST IS ALL!

Jesus, the greatest, most valuable Treasure in the universe, was abandoned on the cross, so that you might be God's special treasure in Christ. Psalm 135:4

On the cross, the Father pursued the Son with anger and condemnation, so that now your heavenly Father, like the Hound of Heaven, is pursuing you relentlessly with goodness and mercy all the days of your life. Psalm 23:6

God the Father and His Son, the Lord Jesus Christ, did all of this ultimately for the praise of His glory and grace! Ephesians 1:6, 12, 14.

So in the face of all failures, heartbreaks, rejections and hopes deferred, be still and know that Christ is all! Rest in Him, enjoy Him, delight in Him above all other delights. And stand secure in the truth of Who Jesus is and who you are in Him by grace through faith!

O Jesus, King most wonderful
Thou Conqueror renowned
Thou Sweetness most ineffable
In Whom all joys are found!

Bernard of Clairvaux

Jesus, my all in all Thou art,
My rest in toil, my ease in pain,
The medicine of my broken heart,
In war my peace, in loss my gain,
My smile beneath the tyrant's frown,
In shame my glory and my crown.
In want my plentiful supply,
In weakness my almighty power,
In bonds my perfect liberty,
My light in Satan's darkest hour,
My help and stay whene'er I call,
My life in death, my heaven, my all.

Charles Wesley

6
"THAT'S MY KING!"
IN THE GOSPEL OF MATTHEW!

The family tree of my King includes whores, hookers, and prostitutes; murderers and adulterers; liars and deceivers, but my King can save them all, change them all, and make all their sins as white as snow!

My King was conceived by the Holy Spirit!
He was born of a virgin!
He came to save His people from their sins!
His name is Immanuel – God with us!
When He was born, a star appeared to lead wise men to worship Him!
He came to shepherd His people Israel!
He's the greater Israel, called out of Egypt to deliver His people from everlasting slavery!

That's my King!

He's the One mightier Whose sandal strap no one is worthy to untie!
He baptizes with the Holy Spirit and with fire!
He alone fulfilled all righteousness!

65

CHRIST IS ALL!

He is God's beloved Son with Whom the Father is well pleased!
He's the greater Adam Who did what the first Adam should have done – He kicked Satan out of the garden of this world!
He's the great Light that dawned to bring His people out of darkness!
He makes those who follow Him fishers of men!
He healed epileptics and paralytics!
He cured those afflicted with various diseases and pains!
He cast out demons!
And He's worthy for us to leave everything precious to us and follow Him wherever He takes us!

That's my King! Do you know Him?!

He's the meekest of the meek!
He hungers and thirsts for righteousness like no other!
He's the most merciful of the merciful!
He's the purest of the purest in heart!
He's the Peacemaker of peacemakers!
Though He's the only one Who ever lived Who deserved no persecution, He was the most persecuted, so that His people might be saved!

That's my King!

He's the Salt of the earth!
He's the Light of the world!
He's the fulfillment of all the law and the prophets!
He's the new and perfect Law Giver!
He's the Treasure of heaven that the human heart longs for!
He's the greatest Gift from heaven we could ever dream of receiving!

That's my King!

He astonished crowds!
He had authority like no other!

CHRIST IS ALL!

He cleansed lepers!
He cooled fevers!
He drove out demons!
He took our illnesses and bore our diseases!

That's my King! I wonder if you know Him today?!

He had no place to live – no place to even lay His head!
He commanded the raging winds and seas to calm down,
and they ceased and became silent!
He's astonishing, frightening, and joy-inspiring all at the
same time!
He forgives and eats with sinners!
He's the all satisfying Bridegroom Who will marry you at
the end of time and fulfill all your desires perfectly!
He raised the dead!
He made the blind to see!
He made the mute to speak!

That's my King!

He's compassionate to the sheep without a shepherd!
He sends His people out to minister and love others in His
name!
He's worthy of more love than you give your own father
and mother!
He's worthy of more love than you give your own sons or
daughters!
He's worthy for us all to lose our lives for His sake!
He's the Teacher of teachers and the Preacher of preachers!
He's the Doer of many mighty works!
He's the only One able to give us rest for our souls!

That's my King!

Are you finding rest for your souls in Him alone today?!

He's the Lord of the Sabbath!
He restores withered hands!
He's the Chosen Servant!

CHRIST IS ALL!

He pleases the soul of the eternal, infinite God!
He proclaimed justice to the Gentiles!
He won't break a bruised reed, and He won't quench a smoldering wick!
He'll bring justice and victory for the glory of the King of kings!

That's my King!

He's the something greater than Jonah!
He's the something greater than Solomon!
He's the brother and son of all those who do the will of His Father in heaven!
He displays in Himself what myriads of prophets and righteous people longed to see!
He opened His mouth in parables and uttered what has been hidden since the foundation of the world!
He's like treasure in a field Who is worthy for us, in our joy, to sell all that we have, so that we can buy that field!
He's the Pearl of great price worthy of all our delight and admiration!
He astonished His people with all His wisdom and mighty works!

That's my King!

He had compassion on the people and fed five thousand with a little food and four thousand too!
He walked on water!
His disciples who knew Him best – His disciples who were Jews and who were only supposed to worship the one and only true God – they worshiped Him because He is God!
People begged merely to touch the fringe of His garment, so that they might be healed!
Because of Him, the mute spoke, the crippled were healthy, the lame walked, the blind could see, and people glorified the God of Israel!

That's my King! Do you know Him?!

CHRIST IS ALL!

He is the Christ, the Son of the living God!
He had to go to Jerusalem and suffer many things, and be killed, and on the third day be raised!
He always set His mind on the things of God and not on the things of man!
He's worthy for us to pick up our cross and follow Him!
He's worth more than the whole world!
He's coming back with His angels in the glory of His Father to repay each person according to what they have done!

Are you ready for the return of the King today?!

He was transfigured on the mountain, His face shone like the sun, and His clothes became as white as light!
He is the One we are to listen to above all others!
He dwells among His people as they gather in His name!
He is more precious than all the riches that this world could offer us!
Everyone who leaves everything to follow Him will receive a hundredfold back in this life and eternal life too!
He's the King Who rode into Jerusalem on a donkey!
God ordained nursing babies to praise Him!
He's the rejected Stone of the builders that has become the Chief Cornerstone!
He's the only one Who ever loved the Lord His God with all His heart, soul, mind, and strength and loved His neighbor as Himself perfectly for the glory of God!

That's my King!

He's the Lord of lords Who will have all enemies put under His feet!
He's the one Instructor!
He's so worthy and His love is so satisfying that to be hated by all nations for His name's sake is a glorious honor!
He will return on the clouds of heaven with power and great glory, and His angels will gather His people from all the nations of the earth!
He's returning at an hour you do not expect!

CHRIST IS ALL!

He will return in His glory, with all His angels with Him, and sit on His glorious throne, separating the sheep from the goats!

That's my King!

Are you ready for the return of the King today?!

He was betrayed, denied, and abandoned by His closest friends!
He was spit upon!
He was beaten!
He was stripped naked!
He was mocked!
He wore a crown of thorns!
He was nailed to a cross!
He was forsaken by God!
He endured the full measure of the wrath of God in place of hell-deserving sinners!

That's my King!

He yielded up His spirit with a loud voice, and when He died the curtain of the temple was ripped in two!
The earth shook, and the dead were raised!
He was buried in the tomb!
But death couldn't hold Him!
He didn't stay dead!
The tomb is empty because He is risen! He's risen indeed!
Now He's alive forevermore to the praise and glory of God!
He has all authority in heaven and on earth!
He's with us always, even to the end of the age!
So we go in His name to make disciples Who follow Him and teach them to obey all that He has commanded!
He's worthy of all our obedience in every area of life forever!
He is not the Father, and He is not the Spirit, but they are all one God in three, distinct Persons all at the same time!

That's my King! That's our King! Do you know Him?!

He that desires anything above Him, equally with Him, or
without Him, shall never obtain Him.

Samuel Ward

The saints . . . would rather lose all than Christ;
they are contented to part with liberty, estate, life,
rather than with Christ.

Ralph Robinson

In all you enjoy, look how much you see of Christ in it.
So far let your delight and esteem be carried out
towards it, and no farther. Do not satisfy yourself
with anything without Christ.

Jeremiah Burroughs

7
"THAT'S MY KING!"
IN THE GOSPEL OF MARK!

He's the Gospel God-Man!
He's the Messianic Savior!
He's the marvelous Gospel!
He's the mightiest of all the mighty!
He's the greater Adam!
He's the greater Israel!
He's the Preacher of preachers and the Teacher of teachers!
He's the One we must trust!
He's the One we forsake all others to have!
He's the irresistible God Who moves us to repentance!
He's the sovereign, gracious God Who attracts us like no other!
He's the One with all astonishing, amazing authority and power!
He's the Healer of the world!

That's my King!

He's the desperate, pleading, prayer Warrior Who prays like no other!
He cast out demons and put the devil on the run!
He's the Clean of cleans!

CHRIST IS ALL!

There's no One like Him!
No one has ever seen anything like Him!
He forgives sins, which only God can do and will cause you
to pick up your mat too!
Jesus said, "Follow Me" and oh what a glorious "Me" He is!
He's the greatest "Me" in all the universe!
He's the greatest "Me" this world has ever seen!
There's no "Me" like this "Me!"
He's the "Me" of Me's, and He is the "He" of He's!
He's the God "Me!"
He's the "Me" Who heals the sick, sets the captives free,
gives sight to the blind, and raises the dead!

That's my "Me!" Do you know Him?!

He's the greatest "Me" that has ever crossed the horizon of
this world!
He's the only "Me" Who saves!
He's the only perfect "Me" Who never sinned!
He's the "Me" Who bore the wrath of His Father on that
cross for sinners!
He's the only "Me" Who conquered sin, death, and Satan
and rose up from the grave!
He's the "Me" Who ever lives to care for, sustain, uphold,
and intercede for His people!
If you have this "Me," you don't need anything else because
He's got it all!
He's the "Me" that makes you see, sets you free, and utterly
satisfies your heart, mind, and soul with unimaginable
glee!

That's my "Me!"

He's the Friend of friends of the sinner of sinners!
He's the Bridegroom of bridegrooms Who alone satisfies!
He's the Feast of feasts worthy to fast for until He returns!
He's the Lord of the Sabbath, the Lord of lords, and the
LORD of all!
He heals the withered hand and gives rest like no other!
He's the Famous One of all famous ones!

CHRIST IS ALL!

He's the greater Moses!
He has the mind of all minds!
He's the strongest of all the strong men!
He conquered and bound the strong man!
He came to destroy the works of the devil!
He's our all-glorious, all-sin Bearer!
He's filled with the Holy Spirit like no other!
He's our Brother like no other from a sinful but blessed mother!
He creates a new family of people from every tribe, tongue, people, and nation with His blood – which is the thickest blood of all!

That's my King! I wonder if you know Him today?!

He's the supreme Sower, Seed, and Soil simultaneously!
He humbles hard hearts like no other!
He's the supreme, sovereign, indomitable Root of Joy Who endured the greatest tribulation and persecution!
He's the Care of cares, the Riches of riches, and the Desire of all desires!
He's the Good-Heart of good-hearts Who causes the Word of God to flourish and bear fruit that will last!
He's the Secret of secrets of the Kingdom of God!
He's the Revelation of the ages that cannot be hidden!
He's the strong, powerful God Who doesn't need us or our help for anything!
He's the Mustard Seed of mustard seeds out growing all the plants of the earth!
He's the ultimate Storm Chaser and the ultimate Storm Crusher all at the same time!
He's the irresistible Lion Tamer and the universe's Reclaimer!
He dries the flow of blood with the cries of His own unquenchable flood!
He's the Death Killer, Life Giver, and Man Thriller!
He's the Teacher, Offender, and Human Soul Mender!

That's my King!

CHRIST IS ALL!

He's worthy to follow in every matter, not to flatter, but all sin to shatter!
He's the reproducing Rabbi with all authority on high Who gives an endless supply!
He has the name that demands fame which we must die to proclaim!
He's the Everlasting Rest Who past the test so we could be forever blessed!
He's the Prophet, Good Shepherd, And Provider Whose strong arms of mercy can't be opened wider!
He's the great I AM HE Who passed by on the sea, makes all fears flee, and sets hearts free!
He's the Healer of all Who reversed the fall and conquers every sickness big or small!
He's the Savior Who cuts bureaucracy, humbles aristocracy, shatters hypocrisy, and rules by autocracy!
He's the Son Who perfectly honored His father and mother and upholds God's Word unlike any other!
His heart is clean, He makes the obscene pristine, and heals the defiled like you've never seen!

He put the Syrophoenician woman to the test
Brought out her best
Healed the possessed
And made the outcast His guest
God's glory to forever express!

He opens ears to hear and mouths to praise
And will only amaze for eternal days!

He more than satisfies all hungry cries and crushed
He dies, but then He'll rise to be our Everlasting Prize!

That's my King! Do you know Him?!

He's the greatest Sign that ever came
All leaven to set aflame
And hard hearts to reclaim
Bringing glory to His most precious name!

CHRIST IS ALL!

He opens blind eyes
And on that cross dies
To triumphantly rise
As our infinite Prize!

His sacrifice more than sufficed
With love and beauty He enticed
And above all He's the glorious Christ!

He crushed the serpent
With passion fervent
As the suffering Servant!

He's the King of self denial
Who endured the hardest trial
To win God's everlasting smile!

He took all our blame
So that for His great name
We would have no more shame
But spread His everlasting fame
And never ever be the same!

His Kingdom came
All power He'd claim
And earth's kings tame
For His great name!

His transfiguration
Revealed His glorification
In a bright sensation
As the beloved Son of all adoration!

He suffered many things
And true salvation brings
By rising King of kings
Now over us He sings!

That's my King! Do you know Him?!

CHRIST IS ALL!

He's the God Who can
Heal uncontrollable man
And forever ban
The devil's wicked plan!

He would be killed
And rise to build
His Church fulfilled
With people thrilled!

He humbled Himself small
As the servant of all
And now stands tall
As the greatest of all!

He received the child
Was meek and mild
Then died reviled
And on this Son His Father smiled!

That's my King!

He has a powerful name
That all must proclaim
Since He took our blame
And death He'd tame!

He was given no cup of water
But went to the slaughter
With God's wrath hotter
So we can drink the living water!

He quenched the fire
And cooled God's ire
On that cross dire
Now He's our all – our great desire!

That's my King!

CHRIST IS ALL!

He's the saltiest salt
Died without fault
Rose up out the vault
To make death halt
So Him we forever exalt!

He never leaves
But to His bride forever cleaves
And all Who trust Him He receives!

He dearly loves His cheating bride
And will not cast her down aside
But for her purity He died!

He was the littlest Child
With greatest righteousness compiled
Yet for our sins He died reviled!

He's rich beyond measure
But gave up His treasure
To fill us with pleasure!

He does the impossibly hard
Through His body scarred
So from His presence we won't be barred!

He died and gave up everything
In order to salvation bring
So we might now forever sing!

He was accused, used, bruised, and spitefully abused
Then rose enthused
So the sting of death would be defused
Satan totally confused
And we would never be refused!

He became the slave of all
And ransomed His people from the fall
By giving the greatest gift of all!

CHRIST IS ALL!

He heals the poor and begging blind
And shows them tender mercies kind
If they will truly trust and find
All joys and hopes in Him combined!

That's my King!

He knows all things
God's rule He brings
And from the crowd "Hosanna!" rings
For He's the humble King of kings!

He spoke and cursed the barren tree
But finally came to set us free
For He's the fruit – come taste and see!

He's the Temple clean
Who drove the robbers from the scene
To grant us grace and peace serene!

He perfectly believed
And holy righteousness achieved
So full forgiveness we've received!

He cried oh Father please forgive
Then died and rose so you could live
And now forgiveness freely give!

He owns all authority on high
False teachers' evil tongues He'd tie
Then speak the truth and for us die!

He's the beloved Son
Whom wicked men would kill and shun
But through His death His work is done
Now He's alive – second to none!

He owns all things
Bold truth He brings
And Caesar bows to the King of kings!

CHRIST IS ALL!

He came from Mary's virgin womb
And faced His Father's wrathful doom
Then resurrected from the tomb
To be our everlasting Groom!

He loved us first
Even though we're sinners worst
Yet for our sake He died as cursed
And now for Him alone we thirst!

He alone fulfilled the greatest commands
Obeying all that God demands
Then took His wrath with nail pierced hands
And conquered death – alive He stands!

That's my King!

He's our sovereign God and LORD
His teachings cannot be ignored
The great crowds heard Him and adored
Believe in Him – there's great reward!

He received the greater condemnation
For prideful lusts of all creation
That He might save from every nation
A humble bride who knows salvation!

He gave up all He had
When He died for sinners bad
And quenched His Father's wrath to add
A righteousness that makes us glad
To end all sin and pain that's sad
And everlasting pleasures add!

He's the Temple we need
And so these buildings He's decreed
Will fall to rubbish flat indeed
And all His warnings we must heed!

That's my King!

CHRIST IS ALL!

He warns of coming judgment doom
So we'll be ready for the gloom
And stand with Him our perfect Groom
For all our foes He will consume!

The end will come, Christ will return
Then raise the dead to fruit discern
The wicked will forever burn
The righteous' joys He did earn
And they for Him will always yearn!

He is LORD and Judge of all
Who said destruction would befall
And yet He'll save all those Who call
So they all will never fall!

His name to all shall be proclaimed
And we must never be ashamed
Since for our sins our King was blamed
So now for Him we are reclaimed!

He endured to the end
But was not saved and did descend
To bear God's wrath and life extend
To those who trust Him as their friend!

That's my King! Do you know Him?!

He was made an abomination
Enduring desolation
While facing our damnation
Then rose for our justification
To save elect from every nation!

He's the highest class
His beauty none can e'er surpass
His every word shall come to pass
And in Him joys we'll amass!

CHRIST IS ALL!

He's the only true and living Christ
So by false christs don't be enticed
To save His elect He alone sufficed
For by the whip He's cut and sliced
Then died and wrapped in grave clothes spiced
But rose alive – the living Christ
Oh great salvation's highly priced
And now hell's fires have all been iced!

He always stayed awake
And made earth quake
When He died to break
And crush the snake
Then rose again new life to make
And His people take
All for love's sake
So now for Him alone we ache!

He's worthy of extravagant devotion
With greatest emotion
For He swallowed God's fury ocean
And rose to the extreme promotion!

He's the Passover Lamb
The Substitute Ram
And the great "I AM"
So we can be children of Abraham!

That's my King!

He's the greatest Man ever born
Though by betrayal He was worn, torn
Silent like a sheep shorn
Treated with scorn
And pierced with thorn
He rose to be salvation's Horn!

CHRIST IS ALL!

His body was broken throughout
And His blood poured out
For us He went without
He's the most devout
Without a doubt
And His work's what this Supper is all about!

His blood was out poured
As the covenant LORD
So we're clean and restored
Through our Christ the Reward
Who's always and only and ever adored!

He's worthy to be remembered, and Him we proclaim
Who took all our shame
And died for our blame
Then rose to great fame
So we're never the same
But live to acclaim
His glorious name!

He never fell away
But always did just what He'd say
Then God did strike the Shepherd slay
His own He won't deny but pay
He died and rose to love display!

That's my King! I wonder if you know Him today?!

He begged His Father to take the cross away
Because with perfect fear He'd pray
With passion every sin He'd slay
And preeminently to God He'd say
You're My greatest joy please stay
Your will be done – I will obey!

CHRIST IS ALL!

He in greatest trial and stress
Would pray His Father God address
Who rules and reigns o'er all distress
Our loving Savior seeks to bless
So to God's will He did say yes!

With a kiss He was sore betrayed
All friends would flee and give no aid
But He our God-Man can't be swayed
He died and in the tomb was laid
He did God's will just as He prayed
Then rose again – our debt's been paid!

He was stripped down naked bare
And men would spit and mock and glare
For our great shame He'd take and wear
Then rise to righteousness declare
And give us clothes that end despair
With Him there's none who can compare!

He's the Son of the Blessed
No testimony against Him past the test
He's the greatest and best
Who they beat and oppressed, undressed
And killed with jest
To remove our sins as far as east is from west
Then He rose with a quest
To leave us at rest
And forever obsessed
With His glory possessed!

That's my King!

He was wickedly denied
By a close friend on the inside
With curse and swearing "no!" He cried
In pride and fear to all He lied
But Jesus faithful went and died
To save His faithless cheating bride!

CHRIST IS ALL!

He's the King of the Jews
And everyone else He'll choose
Silent before those who accuse
Caused Pilate to be amazed and confuse
Then they'd abuse, misuse, and bruise
So that He might be the Everlasting Good News!

He's our perfect substitute
He was killed like a murderous brute
Though He's innocent without dispute
Yet silent and mute
Our sin God did to Him impute
So we'll have and bear His righteous fruit!

He was severely mocked
And on His head they spit and knocked
By death our lowly King was rocked
But in three days they'll all be shocked
He rose and heaven's gates unlocked!

He couldn't carry His cross
To the place of the skull where all seemed loss
The wrath of God He would exhaust
To purchase us at greatest cost!

That's my King! Do you know Him?!

He was King between two thieves
And mocking jeers from all receives
He died to free from all that grieves
He'll save each sinner who believes!

He was utterly forsaken
In darkest cries His heart was shaken
The curtain rent was overtaken
He's God's Son there's no mistakin'
From the grave He would awaken
So we won't ever be forsaken!

CHRIST IS ALL!

He saves and sets the women free
For to His reign they bow the knee
And from His side they did not flee
But His redemption came to see!

He was buried in a rich man's tomb
He took His father's wrathful doom
It seemed that life would not resume
And all men's hearts were filled with gloom
But He would rise – all power assume!

He rose up from the bitter grave
And lives – new life to us He gave
For everyone He came to save
So we could be His holy slave, wholly behave
And Him alone forever crave!

That's my King! That's my King!

O Jesus, Light of all below
Thou Fount of life and fire
Surpassing all the joys we know
And all we can desire!

Bernard of Clairvaux

WHEN Christ uttered, in the judgment hall of Pilate, the
remarkable words: "I am a king," He pronounced a
sentiment fraught with unspeakable dignity and power.
His enemies might deride His pretensions and express
their mockery of His claim, by presenting Him with a
crown of thorns, a reed and a purple robe, and nailing Him
to the cross; but in the eyes of unfallen intelligences, He
was a king. A higher power presided over that derisive
ceremony, and converted it into a real coronation. That
crown of thorns was indeed the diadem of empire; that
purple robe was the badge of royalty; that fragile reed was
the symbol of unbounded power; and that cross
the throne of dominion which shall never end.

J. L. Reynolds

8
"THAT'S MY KING!"
IN THE GOSPEL OF JOHN!

My King was in the beginning!
There never was a time when my King was not!
He always was, and He always will be!
He's the Word!
He's the Word with God!
He's the Word Who is God!
Through Him all things were made that were made!
Without Him nothing was made that was made!
And if you've got Him on your side, then you've got it made!

That's my King!

He's the Life that is the Light of men!
He shines in the darkness, and the darkness cannot overcome Him!
He's the true Light that enlightens everyone!
He made the world!
He came to His own, but His own did not receive Him!
But to those who do receive Him, who believe in His name,
He gives the right to become children of God!
He's the Word that became flesh and dwelt among us!

CHRIST IS ALL!

He's glorious!
He's the only Son from the Father!
He's full of grace and truth!
He brought us grace and truth!
His fullness of grace overflows to us!
He makes God known to us!

That's my King! Do you know Him?!

He's the LORD Whose way had to be made straight!
None of us are worthy to untie His sandal strap!
He's the Lamb of God Who takes away the sin of the world!
He ranks before all of us because He was before all of us!
The Holy Spirit of God remains on Him!
He baptizes with the Holy Spirit!
He's the Son of God!
He's the Messiah!
He's the Good Thing that came out of Nazareth! Come and
see Him! Come and see Him today!

That's my King!

He's the King of Israel!
He opens heaven, so that sinners can be led back to God!
He turned water into wine and kept the best for last!
He cleansed the temple with a whip of cords, and zeal for
God's house consumed Him!
He Himself is God's temple, and zeal for Him ought to
consume us!

Are you consumed with zeal for my King today?!

He's the Temple that was destroyed and raised up in three
days!
He knows all people – their thoughts, motives, and inner
feelings – He knows everything!
Whoever believes in my King has eternal life!
Whoever does not believe in my King is condemned
already!
He's the only begotten Son!

CHRIST IS ALL!

He's the heavenly Bridegroom – the most loving, beautiful, understanding, selfless, satisfying Spouse in the universe!
He must increase, and we all must decrease!
He comes from above!
He's above all!
He speaks the Words of God!
He's loved by the Father Who has given all things into His hand!
Whoever does not obey Him shall not see life, but the wrath of God remains on him!

That's my King! I wonder if you are obeying my King today?!

He's the greatest Gift of God to His people!
He's the Living Water that was poured out for the healing of the nations!
He's the Savior of the world!
He healed the lame!
He's always working for the glory of God and the good of His people!
He does nothing of His own accord, but only what He sees the Father doing!
He gives life to whom He will!
All judgment has been given to Him!
He must be honored just as the Father is honored!
Whoever doesn't honor Him, doesn't honor the Father Who sent Him!
Belief in His Word brings eternal life and passage from death to life!
He commands the dead, and they hear Him and obey!
He came in His Father's name!

That's my King!

He fed five thousand people with five loaves of bread and two fish!
He walked on water!
He gives eternal life!
He's the true Bread from heaven!

CHRIST IS ALL!

He's the Bread of life!
He will not lose anything His Father has given Him, but will raise them up on the last day!
He's the Living Bread that came down from heaven!
Whoever eats Him will live forever!
He's marvelous!
He's the Prophet!
He's the Christ!
He's the Light of the world!
He's not of this world!
He's the great "I AM" in human flesh!
He makes the blind to see!
Never since the world began has there been anyone like Him!
He's the Door of the sheep!
He's the Good Shepherd!
He laid down His life for the sheep!
He's one with the Father!
He's the Resurrection and the Life!
Whoever believes in Him, though he dies, yet shall he live!
And everyone who lives and believes in Him shall never die!

Do believe this about my King today?!

He wept!
He loves like no other!
He raises the dead!
He's worthy for us to fall on our knees and spend all the money and resources that we've ever owned on Him!
He humbled Himself to wash the dirty feet of His disciples!
He's gone to prepare a place for us!
He's the way, the truth, and the life, and no one comes to the Father except through Him!
If you've seen Him, then you've seen the Father!
He is in the Father, and the Father is in Him!
He's the true Vine!
He has overcome the world!
He was denied three times by one of His closest disciples!
His Kingdom is not of this world!

CHRIST IS ALL!

He's the King of the Jews!
He's guiltless!
He's blameless!
He's sinless!
But they crucified Him anyway!
He honored His mother to the very end!
He finished all that was needed for redemption in His
death on the cross!
He rose up from the grave!
He's the Lord and God of all the universe!
He can make all the fish in the sea jump into any net He
wants!
He's merciful to sinful, weak disciples who deny Him three
times!
There are so many things He did that if they were all
written down the world itself could not contain the books
that would be written about Him!

Have you bowed down to Him as your Lord and God
today?!

That's my King! That's my King!

The believer can say: Christ is mine, and I have all things in one, even in Christ, Who is my all and in all. Christ in His Godhead, Christ in His humanity, Christ in His great and finished work, Christ in His mediatorial fulness, must be all in all to the sinner.

Octavius Winslow

"Christ is all and in all" (Col 3:11). He who knows this knows what fully satisfies and cheers. He who knows this best has the deepest and truest peace: for he has learned the secret of being always a sinner yet always righteous, always incomplete yet always complete, always empty and yet always full, always poor and yet always rich.

Horatius Bonar

I wish it were in my power . . . to cry down all love but the love of Christ, and to cry down all gods but Christ, all saviors but Christ, all well-beloveds but Christ, and all soul-suitors and love-beggars but Christ.

Samuel Rutherford

9
"THAT'S MY KING!"
IN THE BOOK OF ACTS!

My King is worthy to have countless biographies written about Him that simply record what He began to do and to teach, let alone record what He's done since He began, what He's doing now, and what He'll do for all eternity!

There aren't enough books in the world to contain the glories of my King! Do you know Him?!

He gave commands to the Apostles through the Holy Spirit!
After His suffering, He presented Himself alive to the Apostles by many proofs!
My King was dead, but now He is alive, and He lives forevermore, never to die again!
My King is worthy to have witnesses testify about Him in Jerusalem, in all Judea and Samaria, and to the ends of the earth!
When He finished His work on earth, He was lifted up to heaven and will return in the same way He departed!

That's my King!

CHRIST IS ALL!

He was attested to you by God with many mighty works
and wonders and signs that God did through Him!
He was delivered up according to the definite plan and
foreknowledge of God!
He was crucified and killed by the hands of lawless men!
But God raised Him up, and He loosed the pangs of death!
It was impossible for death to hold Him!
God would not abandon His soul to Hades nor allow His
Holy One to see corruption!
Through His death and resurrection He has made a way for
us to enjoy fullness of joy and pleasures forevermore at
God's right hand!

That's my King!

God raised Him up and exalted Him to His almighty right
hand!
God has made Him both Lord and Christ!
When He gets a hold of people, they go around selling
everything they have and making sure no one is in need of
anything!
When He gets a hold of people, they spend a lot of time
together, eating together, praying together, and praising
God together because of what their King has done!
In His name, the Apostles baptized thousands for the
forgiveness of sins!
In His name, the Apostles made the lame to walk and leap
and praise the Lord!

That's my King!

He was glorified by the God of Abraham, Isaac, and Jacob!
He was delivered over and denied by wicked sinners in the
presence of Pilate!
He's the Holy and Righteous One Who was denied, so that
the criminal Barabbas might live!
He's the Author of Life, Whom God raised from the dead!
His name, by faith in His name, has made men strong!
Heaven must receive Him until the restoration of all
things!

CHRIST IS ALL!

That's my King! I wonder if you know Him today?!

He's the long awaited, raised up, full of God's Spirit, all powerful, all knowing, all satisfying Prophet, Priest, and King Whom we must listen to, and we must do everything He tells us!
Every soul that does not listen to Him shall be destroyed from the people!
All that the prophets spoke proclaimed the days of my King!
He came to bless us by turning every one of us away from our selfish wickedness!

That's my King!

He's worthy to be preached about, even though you might get thrown in jail!
He's the Stone that was rejected that has become the Chief Cornerstone!
There is salvation in no one else but Him!
There is no other name under heaven given among men by which we must be saved!
He takes uneducated, common men and makes them so bold that they astonish the watching world around them!
He's the kind of King Whom we must open our mouth about no matter what harm anyone threatens against us!

That's my King! Are ready to tell somebody about Him today?!

God exalted Him at His right hand as Leader and Savior to give repentance to Israel and the forgiveness of sins!
His mission will not fail and none of His plans will ever be overthrown by anyone or anything!
He was unceasingly preached everywhere by the Apostles as the Christ!
He stopped the threatening, murderous persecutor of His church – Saul – dead in his tracks and converted him into one of the greatest Christ-exalting theologians and missionaries who has ever lived on the face of this earth!

CHRIST IS ALL!

He is Lord of all!

That's my King!

He was anointed by God with the Holy Spirit and with power!
He went about doing good and healing all who were oppressed by the Devil!
God was with Him!
He was put to death by being hung on a tree!
But God raised Him up on the third day and made Him appear to those who had been chosen by God!
He's appointed by God to be the Judge of the living and the dead!
And everyone who believes in Him receives forgiveness of sins through His name!
My King brings together Jews and Gentiles, slaves and free, men and women, rich and poor, young and old, democrats and republicans, blacks and whites and causes them to join hands and sing in the God-breathed words of the Apostle Paul: "Christ is all! Christ is all! We are all one in Christ, and He is all!"

Now that's my King! Do you know Him?!

Jerusalem and her rulers fulfilled the words of the prophets by condemning my King!
They found no guilt in Him worthy of death, but they killed Him anyway!
They took Him down from the tree and laid Him in a tomb!
But God raised Him up from the dead, no more to return to corruption!
He was given the holy and sure blessings of David that shall never have an end!
Everyone who believes in Him is justified from everything which you could not be justified by the law of Moses!

That's my King!

My King is a King worth risking your life for!

CHRIST IS ALL!

Because He gave His life for us!
His Spirit directs His people where He wants them to preach the Gospel!
In His name, spirits are commanded to flee and they obey!
He is worthy of our thanks and praise, even after being beaten and imprisoned!
He is the One Man by Whom God will judge the world in righteousness!
He taught us that it is more blessed, more satisfying, more full of happiness to give than to receive!
He's worthy to die for!
He takes those who oppose Him, hate Him, and kill His followers and changes them into His greatest supporters, lovers, and witnesses who willingly die for the sake of His name!

That's my King! Are you willing to be a witness for Him today?!

That's my King! That's my King!

My Master has such riches that you cannot count them.
You cannot guess them, much less can you convey
their fullness in words. They are unsearchable!
You may look, and search, and weigh, but Christ
is a greater Christ than you think Him to be
when your thoughts are at the greatest.

My Master is more able to pardon than you to sin, more
able to forgive than you to transgress. My Master is more
ready to supply than you are to ask, and ten thousand
times more prepared to save than you are to be saved.
Never tolerate low thoughts of my Lord Jesus.
Your highest estimates will dishonor Him.

When you put the crown on His head, you will only crown
Him with silver when He deserves gold. When you sing the
best of your songs, you will only give Him poor, discordant
music, compared with what He deserves. But Oh! Do
believe in Him, that He is a great Christ, a mighty Savior.

Great sinner, come and do Him honor by trusting in Him
as a great Savior. Come with your great sins, and your
great cares, and your great wants! Come and welcome!
Come to Him now, and the Lord will accept you,
and accept you without upbraiding you!

Charles Spurgeon

10
"THAT'S MY KING!"
IN THE BOOK OF ROMANS!

My King is the Master of all masters Who set Paul apart for
the Gospel of God!
Everyone should bow their knee to my King and be His
everlasting, always dedicated, humbly submissive slave!
The Gospel of God is all about my King!
God made all kinds of promises in the holy Scriptures from
long ago about His Son, Who was, Who is, and Who shall
forevermore be King of all kings!
He was descended from David according to the flesh!
He's the Son of David Who's greater than David ever was!
He was declared to be the Son of God in power according
to the Spirit of holiness by His resurrection from the dead!
He's Jesus Christ our Lord!
He grants us grace to bring about the obedience of faith for
the sake of His name among all the nations!
He's the reason we have peace with God!

That's my King! I wonder if you know Him today?!

He's the Person through Whom God will judge the secrets
of men's hearts!

101

CHRIST IS ALL!

He's the righteousness of God that's been manifested apart
from the law!
He's the only one Who ever lived a perfectly righteous life
with perfectly righteous faith!
He never suppressed the truth in unrighteousness!
He never exchanged the truth of God for a lie!
He always acknowledged God in everything He did!
He's righteous!
He's good!
He's content!
He's loving!
He's life giving!
He's the Peacemaker!
He's truthful!

That's my King!

He's the preeminent Lover of God!
He's humble!
He obeyed His parents perfectly!
He's the wisest of the wise and eternal life's greatest Prize!
He has the biggest heart of anyone who has ever walked on
the face of this earth!
Glory and honor and peace are due Him because He only
did what was always good!
God judges all the secrets in the hearts and minds of all
people by my King Jesus!
Circumcision was indeed valuable to Him because He did
keep the whole law!
He's not under sin!
He never turned aside from God!
He's worth more than all the joys, pleasures, and riches
this world has to offer!
He only does good!
His throat proclaims an open, empty tomb!
His tongue only speaks what is true!
The honey of the honeycomb is under His lips!
His mouth is full of blessings and sweetness!
His feet are swift to give new life!
In His path is renewal and joy!

CHRIST IS ALL!

His way is peace, and He truly feared God alone like no other!

That's my King! Are you following Him as His disciple today?!

He's the One in Whom we have redemption!
He is the righteousness of God!
The Law and the Prophets bear witness to Him!
He's the only way to be redeemed and regain a right relationship with a holy God!
He was put forward on that cross as an anger removing sacrifice by His own Father!
He displayed to the universe the unflinching, pristine righteousness of His Father in His death on the cross!
By not working but by trusting in my King, you will be counted just as righteous as my King Himself, and you will be accepted in the Beloved!
He was delivered up for our trespasses and raised for our justification!
He died for sinners!
He justifies us by His blood!
He saves us from the wrath of God!

That's my King!

He won for us peace with God!
Through Him we have obtained access by faith into this grace in which we stand, and we rejoice in hope of the glory of God!
He died for the ungodly!
He demonstrates God's love for us in that while we were still sinners, our King died for us!
He reconciled us to God by His death on that cross even though we were His enemies!
His life saves us!
He's the One through Whom we can rejoice!
Through Him we'll reign in life by the abundance of grace and the free gift of righteousness!
Through Him the free gift of God's grace abounds to many!

CHRIST IS ALL!

His one act of righteousness leads to justification and life
for all men!
Through His obedience many will be made righteous!
Because of my King's life, death, and resurrection, where
sin abounds grace abounds all the more!

That's my King! Are you finding your hope and
righteousness in Him alone today?!

Through Him grace will reign, leading to eternal life!
He was raised from the dead by the glory of the Father!
He will never die again!
Death no longer has dominion over Him!
He died to sin and lives to God!
We died with Him, and we died to the law, so that we
might be married to another – Jesus Christ the righteous!
My King delivers wretched men from their bodies of death!
Thanks be to God through Jesus Christ!
The subjects of my King enjoy no condemnation forever,
regardless of what they've done or failed to do in the past!

That's my King!

We can't live in sin anymore because of Him!
We died with Him and have been raised to walk in newness
of life with Him!
We died to sin with Him!
We're alive to God in Him!
Sin will not reign over us because of Him!
We are His slaves!
He is the greatest, best, most loving, most caring slave
Master in the universe!
We died to the law and belong to Him!
He's our Husband Who loves us like no other!
Now since we're one with Him, we can bear fruit for God!
He's the One Who will deliver us from this body of death!
There is therefore now no condemnation for us in Him!
In Him we are set free from the law of sin and death!
He came in the likeness of sinful flesh and was condemned
in the flesh, so that we could be forgiven!

CHRIST IS ALL!

Christ and His Spirit are in us!
The very Spirit Who raised Jesus from the dead dwells in us!
We are fellow heirs with Christ!
Because of Him the sufferings of this present time are not worthy to be compared with the glory that shall be revealed to us!
In Him, EVERYTHING is working together for our good!

That's my King! Do you know Him?!

He was condemned in the flesh, so that the righteous requirement of the law might be fulfilled in us!
He's the greatest Gift the Father could ever give us!
Since the Father didn't even spare His own Son on our behalf, He shall surely with Him also freely give us all things!
He's at the right hand of God always interceding for us for our best and greatest good!
We are being conformed into His image!
Since God in Christ is for us, no one can successfully be against us!
We are more than conquerors through Him Who loves us!
Nothing shall separate us from the love of our King – not tribulation; not distress; not persecution; not famine; not nakedness; not danger; not sword; not death; not life; not angels; not rulers; not things present; not things to come; not powers; not height; not depth; not loneliness; not hard circumstances; not the loss of a spouse; not old age; not singleness; not failing health; not rejection; not failure; not all manner of "impossible to handle situations" in your life; not depression; not hopelessness; not anything else in all creation – none of it – will be able to separate us from the love of God in Christ Jesus our Lord and King!

That's my King! Are you trusting Him with all the circumstances in your life today?!

My King was treated as the rejected One on that cross, so that sinners like you and me might be forever accepted!

CHRIST IS ALL!

My King was made a vessel of God's wrath on that cross, so that sinners like you and me might be vessels of mercy forever!
Whoever believes in my King shall never ever be put to shame!
He's the end of the law for righteousness to everyone who believes!
He's Lord of all!
Through His Word, faith comes that leads to salvation!
He's the only One Who can take away our sins!

That's my King!

He's God over all, blessed forever. Amen!
He's the sovereign God Who has mercy on whom He'll have mercy and Who hardens whom He'll harden!
He's the Stone of stumbling and the Rock of offense!
Whoever believes on Him shall never be put to shame!
He has a zeal for God like no other!
He has His own perfect righteousness and submitted to God's righteousness all at the same time!
He's the end of the law for righteousness to everyone who believes!
You must confess with your mouth that He is Lord, and believe in your heart God raised Him from the dead, and you shall be saved!
Everyone who calls on His name shall be saved!
Faith comes by hearing and hearing through His Word!
He's the Deliverer Who came from Zion!
He banished ungodliness from Jacob!
Through His covenant with us He will take away all our sins!
From Him and through Him and to Him are all things – to Him be glory forever and ever! Amen!

That's my King! Do you know my King?!

Though we are from many different ethnicities, backgrounds, nations, and cultures, we are all one body in my King – we're one in Jesus Christ!

CHRIST IS ALL!

His love is genuine, though He is not loved genuinely in return!
He abhors what is evil!
He holds fast to what is good!
He loves His people with brotherly affection like no other!
He out did and out does everyone in showing honor, even when malicious dishonor is shown toward Him!
He was never slothful but was fervent in spirit and served the Lord like no other!
He rejoiced in hope!
He was patient in tribulation!
He was constant in prayer!
He contributed to the needs of the saints!
He blessed those who persecuted Him, and He loved those who cursed Him!

That's my King! Are you seeking to follow in His footsteps today? And if you're not, I wonder if you know Him?!

He rejoices with those who rejoice, and He weeps with those who weep!
He was not haughty but associated with the lowly and became the lowliest of the lowly on that cross!
He never avenged Himself, but left it to the wrath of God!
He was never overcome by evil, but He always overcame evil with good!
He fed His hungry enemy!
He gave drink to His thirsty enemy!
Whoever serves my King is acceptable to God!
He suffered all the reproaches, pains, and hardships of His people, so that they might be saved!
He made a way for us in all of our diversity to glorify God with one voice!
Through His life, death, and resurrection, He made a way for us to glorify God for His mercy!

That's our King!

He was subject to the governing authorities!
He owed no one anything, and He always loved perfectly!

CHRIST IS ALL!

He loved his neighbor as Himself in perfect holiness and
righteousness!
We belong to Him!
We live to Him!
We die to Him!
He's Lord of the living!
He's Lord of the dead!
In Him there is nothing unclean in itself!
He did not please Himself but "The reproaches of those
who reproached you fell on Him."
He became a Servant to the circumcised to show God's
truthfulness, in order to confirm the promises given to the
patriarchs, and in order that the Gentiles might glorify God
for His mercy!
All that Paul accomplished was Christ in Paul
accomplishing it for the glory of His name!
Jesus Christ is the Author, Subject, Theme, Outline,
Introduction, Body, Conclusion, Structure, Hero, and
Climax of this greatest letter ever written by the power of
the Holy Spirit for the glory of God the Father!

That's my King! That's my King!

May people come away from your ministry (whether it be your preaching, teaching, writing, poetry or whatever) not saying: "Oh what a wonderful preacher, teacher, or writer!" but "Oh what a wonderful Savior!"

Thought from Arnold Dallimore's Spurgeon Biography

The trial of our faith usually comes in the form of affliction. Our jealous Lover uses tests to see if He has our heart. You say, "Lord Jesus, I love you. You are my best Beloved." "Well," says the heavenly Lover, "if it is so, then your precious child will become sick and die. What will you say then?" If you are truthful in what you have said concerning your supreme love for Jesus, you will give up your darling at His call and say, "The LORD gave, and the LORD has taken away, blessed be the name of the LORD."

The more He loves you, the more He will test you. Sometimes He says, "Good woman, I shall take away your husband, on whom you lean, that you may lean the more on Me." I remember Samuel Rutherford, writing to a lady who had lost five children and her husband said, "Oh, how Christ must love you! He would take every bit of your heart to Himself. He would not permit you to reserve any of your soul for any earthly thing." Can we stand that test? Can we let all go for His sake?

Charles Spurgeon

11
"THAT'S MY KING!"
IN THE BOOKS OF
1 AND 2 CORINTHIANS!

My King has a name above all names and everyone who calls upon His name is a saint of the most high God!

The manifold grace of God comes to us in Him!
In Him we are enriched in all speech and knowledge!
He will sustain us to the end, guiltless in the day of His return!
My King didn't send Paul to baptize but to preach the Gospel!
My King's cross is foolishness to those who are perishing, but to us who are being saved it is the very power of God Almighty!
He's the Power of God!
He's the Wisdom of God!
He's our wisdom!
He's our righteousness!
He's our sanctification!
He's our redemption!
He's our only boast!

CHRIST IS ALL!

That's my King! Do you know Him?!

When Paul came to preach to the Corinthians, all he knew was a two point sermon:
Point #1: Jesus Christ!
Point #2: Him Crucified!

He's the crucified Lord of glory!
No eye has ever seen anything like Him!
No ear has ever heard anything like Him!
He's the one and only solid, secure, strong and ever sturdy Foundation!
He will bring to light the things now hidden in darkness!
He will disclose the purposes of every human heart!

That's my King!

He's our Passover Lamb!
In His name we were washed from all our filthy sin!
In His name we were sanctified!
In His name we were justified by the Spirit of our God!
Our bodies belong to Him!
God raised Him from the dead!
Our bodies are members of King Jesus!
My King has assigned each of us a life to lead, and He is in control of every detail of that life!
All the subjects of my King are completely free, no matter what prison conditions they find themselves in!
He's the One Person we should be the most concerned about obeying and pleasing in all things!
All things are through my King!
We exist through my King!
We must submit to, follow, and obey His law with all joy and delight!

That's my King! Are you submitting to my King in all things today?!

He's the spiritual Rock that followed the children of Israel in the wilderness!

CHRIST IS ALL!

He's the life giving Drink that always satisfies your deepest thirst!
He's worthy of exact imitation in every way He calls us to follow Him!
He's the Head of every man!
His body was broken for His people!
The New Covenant was made with His shed blood!
He's Lord!
He speaks with the most beautiful tongues of men and of angels and has perfect love all at the same time!
He has all prophetic powers!
He understands all mysteries!
He has all knowledge!
He has all faith, so as to remove mountains!
And He has perfect love that shows He is everything!
He gave away all that He had!
He delivered His body to be mutilated, beaten, spit upon, stripped naked, hung on a cross, and He did it all in perfect love, suffering the wrath of God, so He gains everything!

That's my King!

He's patient!
He's kind!
He doesn't envy!
He doesn't boast!
He's not arrogant!
He's not rude!
He doesn't insist on His own way!
He's not irritable!
He's not resentful!
He does not rejoice at wrongdoing, but He rejoices with the truth!
He bears all things!
He believes all things!
He hopes all things!
He endures all things!
He never ends!
He's the perfect One Who is, Who has come, and Who will come again!

CHRIST IS ALL!

That's my King! I wonder if you know Him today?!

The story of my King's life, death, and resurrection is THE MATTER OF FIRST IMPORTANCE in the Bible and in the whole world!
He died for our sins in accordance with the Scriptures!
He was buried!
He was raised on the third day in accordance with the Scriptures!
He appeared to many witnesses after His resurrection, proving that He was dead but is now alive forevermore!
He's the firstfruits of those who have fallen asleep!
By Him has come the resurrection from the dead!
In Him, all shall be made alive!
God has put all things in subjection under His feet!
He's the last Adam Who has become a life-giving Spirit!
He's the Man from heaven! – the heavenly Man Who takes away the sin of the world!
God gives us the victory through Him, and in this victory we proclaim: "Death is swallowed up in victory! O death, where is your victory? O death, where is your sting?"
Jesus Christ has given us the victory! Death is dead! Life is given! Christ is risen! And we are free at last!

That's my King!

He's steadfast!
He's immovable!
He's always abounding in the work of the Lord!
He's watchful!
He stood firm in the faith!
He acted like a man – He is the MAN of men!
He's strong!
All that He did, does, and will do is done in the most precious, gentle, and understanding love!
He is so worthy of all our love, joy, and devotion that we should desire His return right now more than we want to experience anything else in this life!
That means . . .
Come Lord Jesus now, before I can grow up!

CHRIST IS ALL!

Come Lord Jesus now, before I get what I want for Christmas!
Come Lord Jesus now, before I fall in love and get married!
Come Lord Jesus now, before I'm able to enjoy children, grandchildren, or great grandchildren!
Come Lord Jesus now, before I'm able to make a great name for myself!
Come Lord Jesus now, before I'm able to get rich!
Come Lord Jesus now, before I'm able to enjoy any other pleasure this life has to offer because You are better than all earthly pleasures! You alone "are fullness and the inexhaustible treasure of incorruptible pleasure!" (Augustine, *Confessions*)

That's my King!

My King Jesus gives grace and peace like no other!
He suffered, so that we might be abundantly comforted!
He is the Yes and Amen of every one of God's very great and precious promises to us!
In Him, God always leads us in triumphant procession!
He is the sweet smelling Aroma of life to God among those who are being saved!
In Him the veil that blinds people's eyes to the truth about God is totally taken away!
He's glorious!
He's the Image of God!
He's Lord!
In His face the light of the knowledge of the glory of God shines forth!

That's my King! Has His light shone forth in your hearts today?!

On that cross He was afflicted in every way and crushed, so that we might be free from affliction forever!
He was persecuted and forsaken, so that we would never be forsaken by the One Who matters most!
He was struck down and destroyed, so that we would be made new!

CHRIST IS ALL!

He has a judgment seat we will all appear before to receive
what is due us for our deeds, whether good or evil!
His love controls us!
He died for all, so that those who live might no longer live
for themselves but live for Him!
He died for their sake and was raised up from the grave!

That's my King!

If you're in Him, you're a new creation – the old has passed
away; behold, all things have become new!
He's the only roadway of reconciliation between God and
man!
He knew no sin, but God made Him sin, so that we might
become the righteousness of God in Him!
He was afflicted, so that you might be forever blessed!
He was beaten, so that you might be forever healed!
He was imprisoned, so that you might be forever set free!
He labored, so that you might forever rest!
He was empty, so that you might be forever full!
He was dishonored, so that you might be showered with
everlasting honor!
He died, so that you might forever live!
He was sorrowful, so that you might forever rejoice!
He was poor, so that you might be made rich!
He had nothing, so that you might possess everything!

That's my King! I wonder if you know Him today?!

Well, though He was rich, yet for your sake He became
poor, so that by His poverty you might become rich!
He sowed more bountifully than anyone, and He will reap
more bountifully beyond our greatest imaginations!
He's the inexpressible gift of God!
He's meek!
He's gentle!
He's humble!
He's bold!
He commands that all our thoughts should obey Him!

CHRIST IS ALL!

He's the heavenly Bridegroom worthy of a pure virgin bride
– the Church!
He's worthy of our pure, undivided, and supreme devotion!
He's a servant of righteousness!
He's a Hebrew!
He's an Israelite!
He's the offspring of Abraham!
And He's dwelling in us!

That's my King!

His grace is sufficient for you in all of your troubles!
His power is made perfect in your weakness!
His power rests upon you in your weaknesses!
He's worthy for us to endure all manner of weaknesses,
insults, hardships, persecutions, and calamities for the
sake of His name!
When we are weak in ourselves, then we are strong in Him!
He's the most powerful of the mighty!
He was crucified in weakness, but He lives by the power of
God!
We are weak in Him, but we will live with Him by the
power of God!

That's my King! That's my King!

Complete in Thee – each want supplied
And no good thing to me denied
Since Thou my portion, Lord, wilt be
I ask no more, complete in Thee.

Aaron Robarts Wolfe

O if I could invite and persuade thousands, and ten
thousand times ten thousands of Adam's sons, to flock
about my Lord Jesus, and to come and take their fill of
[His] love! O pity forevermore that there should be such
an One as Christ Jesus, so boundless, so bottomless, and so
incomparable in infinite excellency and sweetness, and so
few take Him! Oh! Oh! You poor, dry and dead souls, why
will you not come hither with your empty souls to this
huge, and fair, and deep and sweet well of life, and fill your
empty vessels? O that Christ should be so large in
sweetness and worth, and we so narrow, so pinched,
so ebb, and so void of all happiness! And yet men will
not take Him! They lose their love miserably who
will not bestow it upon this lovely One.

Samuel Rutherford

12
"THAT'S MY KING!"
IN THE BOOK OF GALATIANS!

My King gave Himself for our sins to deliver us from the present evil age!
He gives us great freedom that can never be taken away!
He's the great, glorious, beautiful, and all satisfying Object of our justifying faith!
He's the only Object of our justifying faith!
He justifies by His perfect, pure, propitiating works!
In other words, we're saved by His works alone by faith!
Jesus' works are our only hope!

That's my King! Are you resting in His works alone today?!

He loved me and gave Himself up for me!
If you're a Christian, He loved you and gave Himself up for you!
He lives in us!
We live our lives by faith in Him!
Though He did abide by all things written in the Book of the Law and did them, He was cursed by being hanged on a tree as a substitute for sinners!
We are justified by faith alone in Him and not by works of the law!

CHRIST IS ALL!

In Him we enjoy the blessing of Abraham and receive the promised Spirit through faith!

That's my King!

I wonder if you know Him by faith alone today?!

He's the great, singular Offspring of Abraham to Whom God made His promises!
In Him we are all sons of God through faith!
If you've been baptized into Him, then you've put Him on, and you wear Him everywhere you go!
In Him there is neither Jew nor Greek, slave nor free, male nor female, but you're all one in Christ!
If you belong to my King Jesus, then you're children of Abraham and heirs according to the promise!
His Spirit is in your hearts crying "Abba Father!"
Through my King we're no longer slaves but sons!
The very image of my King is being formed in all His people!
He causes the barren woman to rejoice!
He causes the desolate one to be desolate no more!

That's my King!

He's set us free from all evil slavery and made us a slave unto Himself alone!
He's an amazing advantage to us, and if we have Him, we have everything!
In Him all that counts is faith working through love!
He was made sinful flesh on that cross though He knew no sin!
He was made sexual immorality!
He was made impurity!
He was made idolatry!
He was made sorcery!
He was made enmity!
He was made strife!
He was made jealousy!
He was made fits of anger!

CHRIST IS ALL!

He was made rivalries!
He was made dissensions!
He was made divisions!
He was made envy!
He was made drunkenness!
He was made orgies!
And He was cast out of the Kingdom of His Father's
pleasure on that cross, so that you could be saved from all
your works of the wicked flesh!
If you belong to my King, then you have crucified the flesh
with its passions and desires!

That's my King! Are you crucifying your flesh today?!

He's full of love!
He's full of joy!
He's full of peace!
He's full of patience!
He's full of kindness!
He's full of goodness!
He's full of faithfulness!
He's full of gentleness!
He's full of self-control!
And those who belong to Him are full of all that too
because His Spirit lives in them!
His instrument of gruesome execution – that bloody cross
– is the emblem of our greatest and only boast!

Are you boasting in the cross alone today?!

That's my King! That's my King!

Therefore, to you who believe, He is precious

1 Peter 2:7

There is no joy in this world like union with Christ.
The more we can feel it, the happier we are.

Charles Spurgeon

They that have Christ, they have a soul-satisfying portion.
They have the truest pleasures and comforts. Here is to be
found the proper happiness of the soul. Least liable to
accidents and change . . . Here is the best employment for
the understanding . . . Such as have Christ, they have better
and greater riches than others . . . Better honor . . . Far
better pleasures than sensual men. The joys are more
exquisitely delighting than ever was enjoyed by the greatest
epicure [a man who is dedicated to sensual pleasure].
[There are] no pleasures like those that are by the
enlightenings of the Spirit of Christ, the discoveries of the
beauty of Christ and the manifestations of His love.

Jonathan Edwards

13
"THAT'S MY KING!"
IN THE BOOK OF EPHESIANS!

In union with my King, we are blessed with every spiritual
blessing in the heavenly places!
God the Father chose us for salvation in my King before the
foundation of the world!
We were chosen to be holy and blameless before Him!
Only through Him can we be adopted as the beloved sons
and daughters of the living God!
He purchased redemption for us through His blood!
Only in Him can we find forgiveness of sins!
He's got everlasting, unfathomable riches of grace to lavish
upon us for all eternity!
All things are united in Him, whether in heaven or on
earth!

That's my King!

He grants His people an inheritance worth more than ten
trillion worlds with all their riches!
He was raised from the dead with a great and mighty
power!
He was seated at the right hand of His Father in the
heavenly places!

CHRIST IS ALL!

He reigns far above all rule and authority and power and dominion!
His name is above every other name that is named, not only in this age but in the age to come!
All things are under His feet!
He's head over all things!
We can only be made alive with Him by grace through faith!
He is God's riches in mercy to us!
He is the greatest proof and demonstration of God's great love with which He loved us!

That's my King!

Are you grasping the height and width and length and depth of the love of my King for you today?!

All His people are raised up with Him and seated with Him in the heavenly places!
It will take all the coming eternal ages for God to show us the immeasurable riches of His grace in kindness toward us that are found only in my King Jesus Christ!
His blood brings an end to all ethnic hostility!
He's our peace!
He makes all ethnicities, ages, backgrounds, personalities, and preferences one through His death on that cross!
He ended all hostility!
He came preaching peace!
He gives us access in one Spirit to the Father!
He's the Cornerstone!
He's the Temple of God Almighty!
He's making His people into the very dwelling place of God by the Spirit!

That's my King!

He's full and overflowing with unsearchable riches!
Through His church the manifold wisdom of God is being made known to the universe and to the heavenly realms!
He gives us boldness and access to draw near to God!

CHRIST IS ALL!

He dwells in our hearts!
His love for us surpasses knowledge!
He's able!
He's able to do what we can ask or think!
He's able to do all that we can ask or think!
He's able to do more than all we can ask or think!
He's able to do far more than all we can ask or think!
He's able to do far more abundantly than all we can ask or think!

That's my King!

Are you asking and trusting Him to do far more abundantly than all you can ask or think today?!

He's the only One Who ever walked in a manner perfectly worthy of His glorious Father!
He's humble!
He's gentle!
He's patient!
He bore perfectly with all others in love!
He eagerly maintained the unity of the Spirit in the bond of peace!
He's the One Lord!
He gave us the one true faith!
He gave us the only baptism!
He's over all, through all, and in all!
He ascended on high, led a host of captives, and gave gifts to men!
To be like Him and to be full of Him and to grow up in every way into Him is the whole goal of the Christian life!
He's true righteousness!
He's true holiness!
He only and always spoke the truth!
He was angry and did not sin!
He never gave any opportunities to the devil!

That's my King! Are you following in His footsteps today?!

He shared with everyone in need!

CHRIST IS ALL!

Not one corrupt word ever came out of His holy mouth!
He only spoke what was good for building up and gave
grace to those who heard!
He never grieved the Holy Spirit!
He put away all bitterness, wrath, anger, clamor, slander,
and malice!
He's kind, tenderhearted, and forgiving!
He loved us and gave Himself up for us, a fragrant offering
and sacrifice to God!
He's a child of the light Who is the very light of the world!
He's filled with the Spirit!
He loved the church and gave Himself up for her!
He sanctified her!
He cleansed her by the washing of water with the Word!
He will present His bride to Himself in splendor, without
spot or wrinkle or any such thing!
He's the great, glorious, precious, perfect, luscious, loving,
saving, satisfying, benevolent, beautiful Heavenly Spouse
of His blood bought bride – the Church!

That's my King!

And there's no One like Him! I wonder if you're satisfied in
Him alone today?!

He obeyed His parents perfectly in all thoughts, words,
deeds, and feelings!
He obeyed all His earthly masters with fear and trembling
and with a sincere heart!
He's strong in the Lord and in the power of His might!
He put on the whole armor of God!
He triumphantly stood against all the schemes of the devil!
He more than conquered all rulers, authorities, and cosmic
powers over this present darkness!
He defeated all the spiritual forces of evil in the heavenly
places!
He fastened the belt of truth!
He put on the breastplate of righteousness!
He put on the readiness given by the Gospel of peace!

CHRIST IS ALL!

He took up the shield of faith in all circumstances to extinguish all the flaming darts of the evil one!
He took up the helmet of salvation!
He took up the sword of the Spirit, which is the Word of God!
He prayed at all times in the Spirit, with all prayer and supplication!
He kept alert with all perseverance, making supplication for all the saints!
His love is incorruptible, insurmountable, incomparable, incomprehensible, and inconceivable!

That's my King! That's my King!

Has God taken away your only child? He has given His only Son. This is a happy exchange. What need does he have to complain of losses who has Christ? He is His Father's brightness (Hebrews 1:3), His fullness (Colossians 2:9), and His delight (Proverbs 8:30). Is there enough in Christ to delight the heart of God? And is there not enough in Him to ravish us with holy delight? He is wisdom to teach us, righteousness to acquit us, sanctification to adorn us. He is that royal and princely gift. He is the bread of angels (according to Bernard), the joy and triumph of saints. He is "all in all" (Colossians 3:11).
Why then are you discontented?

Thomas Watson

This is amazing indeed! The infinite, everlasting, all-mighty, all-knowing, all-glorious God of all the universe has been absolutely satisfied with Christ in the fellowship of the Holy Trinity from all eternity. Is Christ, then, not enough for us, mere finite vapors? Christ must be all! If He is enough to satisfy the infinite, then He is enough for you, no matter what you lose in this life.

14
"THAT'S MY KING!"
IN THE BOOK OF PHILIPPIANS!

If my King knows you and you know Him, then you are a
saint and set apart for God!

My King is the greatest Master Who has ever blessed the
boundaries of this world!

Every remembrance of Him ought to cause us to explode
with unending praises, thanksgivings, joys, and hallelujahs
unto God!

He will complete every good work in us that He has so
graciously begun!

He yearns for His people with deep, unchanging,
passionate, and everlasting affection!

His love is boundless toward all His people!

He cannot love us more, and He will not love us less! [3]

He always did and always does what is always and only
most excellent!

He's pure!

He's blameless!

He's filled with the fruit of righteousness!

He is, was, and always will be most to the glory and praise
of God!

---

3   From a Michael Card song, *Chorus of Faith*

CHRIST IS ALL!

That's my King!

He's worthy for us to surrender all our freedoms to make
His name known among all peoples!
He inspires confidence in His people!
He's bold!
He's fearless!
He's our righteousness, so that we too can be as bold as a
lion!
He's worthy to be preached about – everywhere, all the
time, preach Him up!
He's the deliverer!
He's honorable!
We ought to seek to honor Him in life and in death!
He's our reason for living!
He's the reason dying is gain because to die and be with
Him is far better than anything this life has to offer!
To be with Christ is far better than any joy, dream, or
pleasure in this world!

That's my King! I wonder if you believe that to die is gain
because of Him today?!

He's glorious!
He's worthy!
He stood firm!
He wasn't frightened in anything by those who opposed
Him!
For His sake we were granted to believe!
For His sake we were granted to suffer!
He's all encouragement!
He's all comfort!
He's all loving!
He's full participation in the Spirit!
He's all affection!
He's all sympathy!
He's complete joy!
He counted everyone more significant than Himself!
He looked out, not for His own interests, but for the
interests of others!

CHRIST IS ALL!

Though He was in the form of God, He did not count
equality with God a thing to be grasped!
He made Himself nothing, taking the form of a slave!
He was born in the likeness of men!
He humbled Himself by becoming obedient to the point of
death, even death on a cross!
Therefore God has highly exalted Him and bestowed on
Him the name that is above every name!
There is no name in heaven or on earth or under the earth
that is greater than the name of my King Jesus!

That's my King! Are you hoping in His name alone today?!

Every knee in heaven and on earth and under the earth will
bow to my King!
All knees will bow either willingly or unwillingly!
All philosophers will bow to my King!
All evolutionists will bow to my King!
All kings will bow to my King!
All evil, murderous dictators will bow to my King!
All religions and religious leaders will bow to my King!
Plato will bow to my King!
Socrates will bow to my King!
Aristotle will bow to my King!
Nietzsche will bow to my King!
Darwin will bow to my King!
All Pharaohs will bow to my King!
All Caesars will bow to my King!
Nero will bow to my King!
Alexander the Great will bow to my King!
Napoleon will bow to my King!
Hitler will bow to my King!
Stalin will bow to my King!
Buddha will bow to my King!
Muhammad will bow to my King!
All presidents, all powers, and all potentates will bow to my
King!
And every tongue will confess that Jesus Christ is Lord, to
the glory of God the Father!

CHRIST IS ALL!

That's my King! Will you willingly bow to Him by faith and confess Him as Lord today?!

He always obeyed!
He works in you both to will and to do according to His good pleasure!
He does all things without grumbling or complaining!
He's blameless!
He's innocent!
He's the preeminent, predominant, precious, perfect Child of God!
He's without blemish!
He shines as the Light of the world!
He holds fast the Word of life!
We've got no one like Him!
He's genuinely concerned for all your welfare!
We owe Him all our allegiance and interest!

That's my King!

He cheers the heart!
He's a brother!
He's a soldier!
He's a worker!
He's a messenger!
He's a minister!
He meets all our needs!
He longs for His people as a Bridegroom longs for His bride on the wedding night!
He shed His blood and died for His bride to save her and to make her holy!
He's the True Circumcision!
He's the True Worshiper of God in the Spirit!
He put no confidence in the flesh!
All the glory belongs to Him!
He was circumcised on the eighth day!
He's of the people of Israel!
He's the Lion of the tribe of Judah!
He's the Hebrew of Hebrews!
He fulfilled the law perfectly!

CHRIST IS ALL!

Zeal for His Father consumed Him!
He obeyed God's law perfectly in every jot and tittle!

That's my King! Do you know Him?!

All the gains and glories, riches and rights, wealth and
women, power and prestige are nothing and less than
nothing compared to the surpassing worth of knowing my
King Jesus!
We ought to suffer the loss of all things and count them as
dung and rubbish in order to gain my King!
Only He grants us a righteousness that can make us right
with God!
He's got the power in His resurrection when God raised
Him from the dead!
He has made us His own!
He will transform our lowly body to be like His glorious
body!
He has mighty power that enables Him to subject all things
to Himself!
He's worthy to rejoice in always!
He's true!
He's honorable!
He's just!
He's pure!
He's lovely!
He's commendable!
He's all excellence!
He's worthy of all praise!
He's worthy of our eternal meditation, contemplation, and
exaltation!
He's got riches in glory that satisfy your deepest longings
and can never be exhausted throughout all eternity!

That's my King! That's my King!

My hope is built on nothing less
Than Jesus' blood and righteousness
I dare not trust the sweetest frame
But wholly lean on Jesus' name.

Edward Mote

Again, He is all in all in the lack of things, whatever it is
that we lack. Do we lack grace, do we lack gifts, do we lack
outward comforts in the world? There is enough in Christ.

It is Christ that is instead of all, that is better than all, and
that will supply all in His due time. Those who know
Christ and have acquaintance with Him, though they have
this and that comfort taken from them, they still
know how to make supply out of Christ.

They have that skill and art and mystery of godliness that
they can make Christ to be all in all in the lack of all, and it
is a great skill and mystery of godliness to know
how to make up all in Christ in the lack of all.

Jeremiah Burroughs

15
"THAT'S MY KING!"
IN THE BOOK OF COLOSSIANS!

My King is the King of a Kingdom named after Himself:
The Kingdom of His Father's Beloved Son!
He's the Image of the invisible God!
He's the Firstborn – the Majestic One – the Preeminent
One over all creation!
By Him all things were created in heaven and on earth!
He created all things visible and invisible!
He created all thrones, dominions, rulers, and authorities,
and He rules over them all!
All things were created through Him and for Him!
He's before all things!
In Him all things hold together!

That's my King!

He's the Head of the body which is His blood bought Bride:
the Church!
He's the Beginning!
He's the Firstborn from the dead!
He's preeminent in everything!
In Him all the fullness of God was pleased to dwell!

CHRIST IS ALL!

Everything, whether on earth or in heaven, is being
reconciled to God through Him!
He has made peace by the blood of His cross!

That's my King! Are you enjoying peace with God through
the blood of His cross today?!

He has reconciled alienated, hostile-minded, evil doers
back to God in His body of flesh by His death!
If you continue in the faith, stable and steadfast, not
shifting from the hope of the Gospel, He will present you
holy and blameless and above reproach!
He's in you!
He's your hope of glory!
He's Who we preach, what we preach, why we preach, and
without whom we'd have nothing at all to preach!
To be mature in Him is the final goal of every one of His
blood bought children!
He enables us to live for Him by powerfully working all His
energy within us!

That's my King!

In Him are hidden all the treasures of wisdom and
knowledge!
In Him the whole fullness of deity dwells bodily!
He's the head of all rule and authority!
God powerfully worked in Him and raised Him from the
dead!
In Him God disarmed the rulers and authorities and put
them to an open shame by triumphing over them!
The substance of all Old Covenant religious practices
belongs to Christ!
He's seated at the right hand of God!
He's your life!
He brings peoples from every class, ethnicity, background,
and status together and makes them one in Himself!
He's all and in all!

That's my King! I wonder if He's your all in all today?!

CHRIST IS ALL!

He's God's chosen One!
He's holy and beloved!
He's compassionate!
He's kind!
He's humble!
He's meek!
He's patient!
He's forgiving!
Above all He's loving!
His peace should rule in your hearts!
His Word should dwell in you richly!
In His beautiful name you should do everything, whether
in word or in deed!

That's my King! That's my King!

I want nothing but this Christ. He shall be a Treasure so great to me that everything else will seem dung to me. He shall be a Light so great to me that, having apprehended Him by faith, I do not care to know whether there is a law, sin, and any righteousness or unrighteousness in all the world. For what is everything in heaven and on earth compared with the Son of God, Jesus Christ, my Lord, Who loved me and gave Himself for me?

Martin Luther

Jesus is very, very great . . . Is there anything great in the world that excites you, that you go out of your way to see or hear or experience? Christ made it! He thought it up. And He is ten million times greater in every respect – whatever it is, except sin. If you took all the greatest thinkers of every country and every century of the world and put them in a room with Jesus, they would shut their mouths and listen to the greatness of His wisdom. All the greatest generals would listen to His strategy. All the greatest musicians would listen to His music theory and His performance on every instrument . . . Jesus is very great. Words fail us to describe how great Jesus is. There is nothing that Jesus cannot do a thousand times better than the person you admire most in any area of human endeavor under the sun . . . You admire politicians? – you admire physically beautiful people? – you admire intelligent people? – you admire musicians? – you admire sports? . . . Anything that you admire Jesus Christ can do ten thousand times better!

John Piper

16
"THAT'S MY KING!"
IN THE BOOK OF REVELATION!

The book of Revelation is the revelation of my King!

Those who hear and keep the revelation of my King shall
be unimaginably happy and satisfied throughout all
eternity!

My King is the faithful Witness!
He's the Firstborn from the dead!
He's the Ruler of all the kings of the earth!
He loves us!
He's freed us from our sins by His blood!
He's made us a kingdom and priests to His God and
Father!
To Him be glory and dominion forever and ever! Amen!

That's my King! Are you eager to give Him glory today?!

He's coming with the clouds, and every eye will see Him,
even those who pierced Him!
All the tribes of the earth will wail on account of Him!
He's the Alpha and the Omega!

CHRIST IS ALL!

He's the Lord and God!
He's the One Who is and Who was and Who is to come!
He's the Almighty!

That's my King!

In Him is patient endurance!
He's worthy for us to be imprisoned and outcast, never to
be heard from again on account of His name!
He's the Son of Man!
He wears the most beautiful clothes you have ever seen or
imagined!
His eyes are like a flame of fire!
His voice is like the roar of many waters!
He sovereignly holds His blood bought churches in His
righteous, right hand!
From His mouth come a sharp, two-edged sword!
His face is like the sun shining in full strength!

That's my King! I wonder if you know Him today?!

If you saw my King, you would fall down to the ground as if
you were dead!
But He'd tell you not to fear! Because though He's not safe,
He's real, real good![4]
He's the First and the Last!
He's the Living One!
He died, but behold, now He's alive forevermore!
He holds full command of the keys of Death and Hades!
He knows everything every person on earth has ever done,
thought, felt, or said!
He don't need a list; He ain't checkin' it twice; and He
knows we've all been naughty and not nice!
So He came to save us from our sins through His perfect
sacrifice!
Which will always, only, and forevermore suffice!

---

4   This thought comes from C. S. Lewis in *The Lion, The Witch,
    And The Wardrobe.*

CHRIST IS ALL!

That's my King!

He's worthy of our first love, our greatest love, and all the love that we can give and more!
Because He conquered, He grants to His conquerors to eat of the tree of life in the paradise of God!
His conquering followers will not be hurt by the second death!
His conquering followers will be given some of the hidden manna and a new name!
His conquering followers will be given authority over the nations and the morning star!
His conquering followers will be given beautiful, white garments, and their names will never be blotted out of the book of life but will be confessed before His Father and the angels!
His conquering followers will be made a pillar in the temple of His God, and He will write on them the name of His God!
His conquering followers will sit with Him on His throne, just as He conquered and sat down on His Father's throne!

That's our King! Do you know Him?!

He has the seven spirits of God and the seven stars!
He's the Holy One!
He's the True One!
He has the key of David!
He opens, and no one will shut!
He shuts, and no one will open!
He's the Amen!
He's the faithful and true Witness!
He's the Beginning of God's creation!
Though we are wretched, pitiful, poor, blind, and naked; He came to make us rich, prosperous, and in need of nothing because we have Him as our great Joy and Treasure!

That's my King! Are you finding Him to be your all sufficient Joy and Treasure today?

CHRIST IS ALL!

He's the Gold we need to be rich!
He's the white, spotless Garment we need to be clean!
He's the Salve we need for our eyes, so that we can see!
He disciplines those He loves!
He stands at the door and knocks and calls us all to come
in to Him to eat, drink, and be eternally saved, safe, and
satisfied![5]

That's my King!

He's the Lion of the tribe of Judah!
He's the Root of David!
He conquered!
He's worthy to take the scroll of history and all God's
decrees to open its seals!
He's the slain Lamb of God Whose blood ransomed people
for God from every tribe, language, people, and nation!
He's worthy to receive power and wealth and wisdom and
might and honor and glory and blessing!
To Him and to His Father are blessing and honor and glory
and might and worship forever and ever!

That's my King!

When my King comes back, and be sure of this – He will
come back! – those who have not bowed the knee to Him
by faith will cry out for the mountains and rocks to fall on
them to hide them from His almighty wrath!

Salvation belongs to our King!
His blood makes our dirty robes as white as snow!
Because of Him, we'll hunger no more!
Because of Him, we'll thirst no more!
Because of Him, the sun shall not strike us and the heat
shall not scorch us!

---

5   John Piper used this phrase in the funeral sermon he gave for
    his father on March 9, 2007.
    http://www.desiringgod.org/conference-messages/funeral-
    message-for-william-s-h-piper Accessed 21 JAN 2015.

CHRIST IS ALL!

He will be our Shepherd, and He will guide us to the
springs of living water!

That's my King! Is He your Good Shepherd and Living
Water today?!

The kingdom of the world will become His kingdom!
He shall reign forever and ever!
He conquers every power that's against Him!
He's the King of kings and the Lord of lords!
His name is Faithful!
His name is True!
He judges in righteousness and makes war on His enemies!
On His head are many crowns!
He's clothed with a robe dipped in blood!
And His name is The Word God!

That's my King!

He's the Temple of the living God!
He's the Light in which the nations walk!
From His throne flows the river of the water of life that is
bright as crystal!
He's returning to repay everyone according to what he has
done!
He's the Alpha and the Omega!
He's the First and the Last!
He's the Beginning and the End!
He's the Root and descendant of David!
He's the bright and morning Star!
He's surely coming back soon!
Oh come Lord Jesus! Come quickly!

That's our King! Are you living in such a way so that His
return might be hastened today?!

That's my King! That's my King!

. . . to a poor hungry sinner, Jesus Christ is everything.
He is a home for his [homelessness]; [clothes] for his
nakedness; food for his hunger; light for his darkness;
liberty for his bondage; joy for his despair. He is his
Heaven upon earth and his Heaven in Heaven!

Charles Spurgeon

The man who has God for his treasure has all things in
One. Many ordinary treasures may be denied him, or if
he is allowed to have them, the enjoyment of them will
be so tempered that they will never be necessary to his
happiness. Or if he must see them go, one after one, he
will scarcely feel a sense of loss, for having the Source
of all things he has in One all satisfaction, all pleasure,
all delight. Whatever he may lose he has actually lost
nothing, for he now has it all in One, and he
has it purely, legitimately, and forever.

A. W. Tozer

17
"THAT'S MY KING!"
WHO'S THE SUPREME SOWER, SEED, AND SOIL SIMULTANEOUSLY!

He's the supreme Sower, Seed, and Soil all at the same time!

He's the Sower who sows better and broader, longer and more lavishly, deeper and with more delight, and more effectively and everlastingly than any sower who's ever lived!

He's the Sower of sowers!

He's the only Sower Who can make the seed from nothing, plant the seed in the most fallow ground, and make it grow to produce the most amazing harvest just as He pleases!

He can make the hardest of soil soft; keep all the birds away from His seed; make the rockiest of soils harvestable; kill every thorn; and make all soil good for His own glory!

He penetrates the hardest of hearts!

He destroys all the works of the Devil!

He plants joyful roots that last forever in the face of all manner of tribulations and persecutions, so that no one ever falls away!

He conquers every worldly care by carrying them on His own back, so that you don't have to!

CHRIST IS ALL!

He's more precious than all the riches of 10 trillion universes!
He's the Desire of all desires and better than them all combined!

That's my King!

He always gets the exact harvest He wants from all His sowing efforts!
He forever, always, and only sows what is good, true, right, helpful, loving, wise, and life changing!
He sows true light into the hearts of men and women, boys and girls!
He sows joy into the heart that never goes away or diminishes but only grows more and more intense throughout all eternity!
He sows to sinners of all stripes, shapes, and sizes and to sinners of all degrees of deadness and despicableness!
And if they repent and believe in Him, they shall all be saved!
He sows more bountifully than the most bountiful of the bounty!
He has a hand in the sowing of every faithful sower who has ever lived!
He sowed to the Spirit in perfect righteousness, so that we might sow His Word in His name – the name above all names!
He sowed righteousness, reaped mercy, sought the LORD, and rained righteousness upon all those who would ever turn from their sin and trust in Him!
He sowed in tears like great drops of blood in His wrath bearing death, but He reaps in even greater shouts of joy over the innumerable harvest of saved souls through His resurrection from the dead!

That's My King! Do you know Him?!

He's the Seed Who can plant Himself, fertilize Himself, water Himself, shine light on Himself, grow Himself, and bloom, flourish, and harvest Himself all by Himself!

He's the self-sufficient Seed of the universe!
He doesn't need you or me to plant Him or to do anything
for Him!
But He loves us, so He uses us to spread His matchless
fame and glory all around the world!
He IS the Seed of seeds!
He's the Seed of the woman Who crushed the head of the
serpent!
He's the primary, predominant, prevailing Seed of
Abraham through Whom all of God's promises are yes and
amen!
He Himself is the Seed He sows, so that if anyone hears His
voice and believes in Him they shall be saved!
He's the Word made flesh Who dwelt among us Who alone
can save us from God's wrath to come!
Long ago, at many times and in many ways, God sowed the
Seed to our fathers by the prophets, but in these last days
He has sown the Seed by His Son, Whom He appointed the
heir of all things, through Whom He also created the
world!
Though heaven and earth will pass away, His Seed will
never pass away!
He's the preeminent grain of wheat that died and was
buried in the earth for three days, but then was raised up
from the grave with power in order to bear much
everlasting fruit!

That's my King!

He's the Good Soil Who always heard the Word of God,
always trusted the Word of God, always loved the Word of
God, always obeyed the Word of God, always delighted in
the Word of God Who Himself is the very Word of God
Himself!
He defeated the Devil when the Devil tried to snatch up the
Good Seed away from Him and use it against Him!
He never let His heart become hard but was always quick
to receive the pure milk of the Word!

The Word took deep root in His heart, and He stored it up in His heart, mind, and soul, so that He would never sin against God in the smallest degree!
The cares of this world never distracted Him from fulfilling His God-given mission!
The deceitfulness of riches never deceived Him because He IS the riches of this universe all in one Man: the God-Man!
He never desired any other thing besides perfectly doing the will of His Heavenly Father!
On the cross He was made sin, though He knew no sin, so that we might become the righteousness of God in Him!
He was made hardness of heart toward God and crushed on that cross, so that you could be forgiven of all your hardness of heart and receive a soft heart that trusts, loves, and lives for God forever!
His root with the Father was cut off, and His supreme joy in the Father's presence was abolished on that cross, so that you would never be severed from the Father but enjoy fullness of joy and pleasures forevermore in His presence for all eternity!
He was made the cares of this world and crushed on the cross, so that you could be forgiven for caring more about this world than about God!
He was made the wicked love of money on that cross, so that you could be forgiven for loving money more than God!
He was made the evil desires for other things on that cross, so that you could be forgiven for desiring toys, treats, sex, songs, spouses, power, pleasure and anything else that you might desire more than God Himself!
He died and spent three days and three nights in the heart of the soil but was raised up from the dead to never die again!
He bore so much fruit that if it were all written about, I suppose the world itself could not contain the books that would be written!

CHRIST IS ALL!

One day He will renew this earth with all its soil and bring into reality the new heavens and the new earth where there will be no more sin, no more pain, no more death, and no more tears!

That's my King! That's my King!

You [God] are fullness and the inexhaustible treasure of incorruptible pleasure . . . You are my true joy if I submit to you . . . the only sure source of pleasure . . . Enable me to find rest in You oh God! Grant me that You come to my heart and intoxicate it, so that I forget my evils and embrace my one and only good, Yourself!

Augustine

Christians might avoid much trouble and inconvenience if they would only believe what they profess, that God is able to make them happy without anything else. They imagine that if such a dear friend were to die, or if such blessings were to be removed, they would be miserable, whereas God can make them a thousand times happier without them. To mention my own case, God has been depriving me of one blessing after another [he was on his death-bed when he wrote this], but as each one was removed He has come in and filled its place. And now, when I am cripple and not able to move, I am happier than ever I was in my life before or ever expected to be; and if I had believed this twenty years ago I might have been spared much anxiety.

Edward Payson

18
"THAT'S MY KING!"
WHO MAKES THE DIRTIEST CLEAN!

He made both the clean and unclean animal, but
proclaimed all foods acceptable through His life infallible
and radical giving us joy in God maximal!
He's the clean Place Who makes all the ground around
Him clean space no matter how base by His amazing grace!
He's the cleanest and keenest Who's furtherest from the
meanest!
He's clean like you've never seen, perfect in every gene, the
purest, holiest Scene, more majestic than any queen!
In His blood take a bath to save you from God's wrath and
lead you down salvation's everlasting path!

That's my King!

His life, death, and resurrection cry: "Atone!" For this
purpose His Word was sown to break our hearts of stone
that we might never be alone but truly be known by the
God Who saved us for His own!
He heals all our diseases and seizes what pleases through
the cross alone His Father He appeases!

CHRIST IS ALL!

If you want to be clean, don't wait seven days, there are no delays, just turn your gaze to His face full of praise!
You can be pure, for His victory is sure through which He Himself is the cure!
He came to clean the inside of the cup – to show us down is the new up, so that with God we might forever sup!
His blood sprinkles clean hearts from the beginning He starts and doesn't stop till He cleanses all parts!
He became unclean on that cross where everything He lost as He counted the cost – His love we can never exhaust though we're tossed, bossed, and by all manner of trials crisscrossed!

That's my King! I wonder if you know Him today?!

Through His death on the tree He makes dirt of every degree flee, just make your plea and come and see how you can be set free by the great One in Three!
He'll help you do drugs and alcohol no more; they've left your life sore; they're only a bore; His law you ignore; from your true life they tore; but He can restore and make you adore – His goodness and mercy forevermore!
If to sexual addiction you're chained, His blood was drained that you could be reclaimed and have your purity regained and enjoy eternal life unstained!
If you've faced abuse in the past, His love and grace are so vast, He can heal what's amassed and your past He'll recast at last into joy and peace unsurpassed!
If to pride you've not yet died, He was pierced in His side to make you His humble bride with Him to forever abide!

That's my King!

He'll set you free from the love of money – on the cross He got bloody to show you His love is sweeter than honey and brighter than sunny!
If your anger you can't control, He'll make you whole 'cause He gave up His soul, therefore He's worthy to open the scroll with God's glory as His most holy goal!

CHRIST IS ALL!

No matter what your sin whether you're addicted to skin,
gin, what has been, or all manner of darkness within –
Jesus can win!
For He didn't just die when He let out the cry into the dark
sky seen by every eye!
He said: "It is finished!" and His glory would never be
diminished!
He rose up from the grave, so that you He might save,
make you brave, and cause you to Him alone crave!

That's my King! That's my King!

Apart from Christ let nothing dazzle you.

Ignatius

The secret of holiness is heart-occupation with Christ. As we gaze upon Him we become like Him. Do you want to become like Christ? . . . Let the loveliness of the risen Lord so fill the vision of your soul that all else is shut out.

Harry Ironside

To be brief, we must be sure of the infinite good that is done to us by our Lord Jesus Christ, in order that we may be ravished in love with our God and inflamed with a proper zeal to obey Him, and keep ourselves strictly in awe of Him, to honor Him with all our thoughts, with all our affections, and with all our hearts.

John Calvin

19
"THAT'S MY KING!"
WHO'S THE RISING WHO
SAVES TO THE UTTERMOST!

He's the Rising of risings of this world!
At the first sun rise this universe has ever witnessed, He was there making it all happen!
He upholds every sun rise by the Word of His power!
Every rising of the sun ought to remind us of the rising Son of Righteousness Who brings healing in His wings to all who fear His name!
From the rising of the sun to its setting His name will be great among the nations!
From the rising of the sun to its setting His name is to be praised!
From the rising of the sun and from all directions, there is none besides Him; He is God in the flesh, and there is no other!
His name shall be feared from the north, south, east and west, and His glory from the rising of the sun!
He rises up to plead mercy for His children, and there's no condemnation for those who put their faith in Him!

That's my King! Do you know Him?!

CHRIST IS ALL!

Those who are righteous by faith in Him may fall down
seven times, but each time they will rise again because of
His almighty power which works so mightily in them!
At the end of time when He rises to terrify those who have
not trusted in Him, sinners will cry out for the mountains
to fall on them to shield them from His everlasting fury!
His tongue rises to defend His children against all the
accusations of the Devil!
He's the star that came out of Jacob and the King that rose
out of Israel Who shall crush all of His and our enemies
and put them under His feet!
He's the Morning Star Who rises in the hearts of His blood
bought people!

That's my Kingly Star! I wonder if He's risen in your hearts
today?!

He has caused our enemies to rise against us only to be
defeated before us!
They shall come out against us one way, but run from us
seven ways!
He rises to pursue us with goodness and mercy all our
days!
When He was born all nations came to His rising light!
Kings came to the brightness of His rising over the stable
in Bethlehem!
He died and rose again, so that death, the world, the flesh,
and the Devil shall die to never rise again forevermore!
He causes those who trust Him to rise and stand upright –
free from all condemnation forever!
He's risen up and come to help us for the sake of His
steadfast love!
He poured Himself out for the hungry and satisfies the soul
of the afflicted, and His light has risen in darkness!
Because He is risen, we can say with the prophet Micah:
"Rejoice not over me, O my enemy; when I fall, I shall rise;
when I sit in darkness, the LORD will be a light to me. I
will bear the indignation of the LORD because I have
sinned against Him, until He pleads my cause and executes
judgment for me.

He will bring me out to the light; I shall look upon His righteousness!"
He made the cripple and unraisable to arise and walk!
He raises the poor from the dust and lifts the needy from the ash heap!
He raises up the needy out of affliction and makes their families as numerous as the stars of the sky!
He raises up all who humble themselves and are bowed down!
He's the Prophet raised up by God Who is the Greater Moses!
He's the Faithful Priest God raised up to do according to all that is in His heart and mind!
He's the offspring of King David raised up to be the Greater David and everlasting King of His people!
Remember Jesus Christ, risen from the dead, the Offspring of David!
May we rise and go and seek Him Whom our souls love!

That's my King! Is your soul in love with Him today?!

His own Father's anger rose up against Him in full strength on that cross until He died, and then the Father raised Him from the dead as the revered, relished, rising, resurrected Redeemer Who alone saves all those who repent and believe in Him!
Though your sins have risen higher than your heads, and your guilt has mounted up to the heavens, His rising casts all your sins into the depths of the sea; though your sins were as scarlet they have become as white as snow; as far as the east is from the west, so He has removed your sins from you, and He remembers them no more!
When you trust in Him, the glory of the LORD has risen up to you as you see the light of the knowledge of the glory of God in the face of Jesus Christ!
He is not in the tomb; He is risen as He said!
He causes feelings and sounds of joy to rise from all the hearts and mouths of those who truly know Him!
He's the Righteous Branch raised up for David Who is the LORD God our righteousness!

CHRIST IS ALL!

He's so great He causes shouts to rise in our hearts, and
our mouths cannot be silent!
He raises up dead, dry bones and makes them new, living
creatures who live for God!
He's able to raise up stones and make them children of
Abraham!
He's the Rising Who heals the sick, raises the dead,
cleanses lepers, and casts out demons!
Those who truly know Him will celebrate His resurrection
everyday and not just once a year!

Please come on up to this Rising today, next Sunday, and
everyday, for He is worthy!

He's the Temple that was destroyed and raised up in three
days!
Everyone who looks on Him and believes in Him shall have
eternal life, and He will raise him up on the last day!
He's the Horn Of Salvation raised up for everyone who
would ever turn and trust in Him!
God raised Jesus up from the dead, loosing the pangs of
death, because it was not possible for Him to be held
captive by death!
He's the Author of Life Whom God raised from the dead!
He's the "Raised Up Servant" sent to you to bless you by
turning every one of you away from your wickedness!
He was delivered up for our trespasses and raised for our
justification, no longer to see corruption!
He will never die again because death no longer has
dominion over Him!
The Spirit of Him who raised Jesus from the dead dwells in
you, so that you might bear fruit for God and live for His
glory!
If you confess with your mouth that Jesus is Lord and
believe in your heart that God raised Him from the dead,
you will be saved!
God, being rich in mercy, because of the great love with
which He loved us, even when we were dead in our
trespasses and sins, made us alive together with Christ –
by grace you have been saved – and raised us up with Him

and seated us with Him in the heavenly places in Christ
Jesus, so that in the coming ages He might show the
immeasurable riches of His grace in kindness toward us in
Christ Jesus!
We are waiting for our King from heaven, Whom God
raised from the dead, Jesus Who delivers us from the
wrath to come!

That's my King! That's my King!

It is as if the only pleasure and intimacy in this life that comes close to anticipating the pleasure of the church and her Lord being perfectly united on the last day is the sexual union of a good marriage.

D. A. Carson

God created us with sexual passion so that there would be language to describe what it means to cleave to Him in love and what it means to turn away from Him to others . . . God made us powerfully sexual so that He would be more deeply knowable. We were given the power to know each other sexually so that we might have some hint of what it will be like to know Christ supremely.

John Piper

One of the greatest ironies of the postmodern West might be this: that great symbol of pleasure in our culture for which it (consciously or not) most emphatically rejects God – sex – is the very thing God has given humanity so that it might have an analogy, a category, a language for knowing what the unadulterated enjoyment of Him will be like in glory (see Eph. 5:22-33). In other words, we reject God for sex, but sex is exactly what He's given us in order to faintly grasp the experience of a perfect union with Him.

Jonathan Leeman

20
"THAT'S MY KING!"
ON VALENTINE'S DAY!

My King is the Lover of all lovers of all time!
He's the Valentine of valentine's!
His love far surpasses your ability to even understand or
comprehend how much He loves!
His love surpasses knowledge!
His love is the only love that satisfies the deepest longings
of the human heart!
His love was enough to satisfy the infinite, everlasting
Father for all eternity – so how much more must it satisfy
your finite, frail human heart?!
He's enough for God! Oh how much more than enough is
He for you!
He loved so much
that He took on human flesh
lived a perfect life
died the most horrifying death this universe has ever seen
suffered the pains of myriads of hells in place of sinners
rose up from the grave triumphant over sin, death, and
Satan
and ever lives to plead mercy for His beautiful, blood
bought Bride!

CHRIST IS ALL!

That's my all-satisfying King!

My King is more precious than more than 999 trillion
universes of gold!
And every other good gift in this life compared to Him is
worth less than a penny!
He commands me to hate everything else in comparison to
the love I must have for Him!
And He's worthy of all that kind of love and all that kind of
hate!
He's more valuable than the most precious gold and the
most priceless diamond!
His value far exceeds 999 trillion worlds with all their
riches and pleasures!
Whatever you love and value most in this life – Jesus
exceeds that value in ways that are incomparable!

That's my King! Do you know Him?!

He's the King of all beauty!
He's the Beauty of beauties!
He's more beautiful than the most beautiful sunset because
He made the sunset!
He's more beautiful than the most breathtaking scenery in
the universe because He made the universe and upholds it
by the Word of His power!
He's more beautiful than the most stunning flower of the
field because He made them all and sustains them all!
He's more beautiful than all the starry hosts and the most
amazing phenomenon in the galaxy because the heavens
are telling His glory, and He placed all the stars in the
heavens to magnify His own beauty!
He's more beautiful than the most gorgeous woman who
has ever crossed the horizon of this world because
she is created, but He created her
she is sinful, but He is perfect
she is finite, but He is infinite
she is the image, but He is the real thing!

CHRIST IS ALL!

If the art work of woman is so amazingly, breathtakingly, gloriously, speechlessly beautiful (and she is!), oh how much more amazingly, breathtakingly, gloriously, speechlessly beautiful must my King the Artist be?!
Oh He is so beautiful!
More beautiful than we could ever dream or imagine!

That's my King! That's my Lover! Do you know Him?!

He's the Lover Who will never let you down!
He always desires you just how you want to be desired!
He always gives you just what you need!
He's always excited to be with you!
He always delights over you!
He sings over you with loud shouts of great joy!
He always passionately and purposefully pursues you with passionate, pleasing pleasures!
He not only loves you like no other, but He makes you feel loved like no other!
He's always the most desirable of all lovers!
You'll long for Him like you've longed for no one else!
He'll take your breath away!
He'll make you jump and shout and turn all about!
He'll fill your stomach with joy and butterflies like no one you've ever met!
You'll be so in love with Him that your body would explode if He didn't first give you a new, glorified body!
He alone gives you the deepest, best, and longest lasting intense pleasures that have ever crossed the horizon of this world!
The most intense pleasures this world or any other lover in this world could ever offer you are only tiny candles compared to the blazing, infinite sun of our pleasure giving, ravishing, all-satisfying God!
In His presence is fullness of joy, and at His right hand are pleasures forevermore!
He will give you pleasures that are out of this world for all eternity beyond what you could ever dream or imagine!

That's my King! That's my King!

As one has aptly and truly stated the case, it is not faith that saves but faith in Jesus Christ; strictly speaking, it is not even faith in Christ that saves but Christ that saves through faith . . . The specific character of faith is that it looks away from itself and finds its whole interest and object in Christ. He is the absorbing preoccupation of faith.

John Murray

Christian, do you feel as if you are nothing? It matters not, for you are enough in your Jesus. Are you dark? He is a fountain of light. Are you dead? He is a fountain of life. Are you poor and low, weak in knowledge, in faith, in love, in patience? He is a treasure of all grace. And whatever He is, He is for you! Is He wise? He is wise for you. Is He holy? He is holy for you. He is meek, He is merciful, humble, patient for you. He is strong, rich, and full for you. Bewail your own poverty and weakness, but bless yourself in your Lord, for He is rich, righteous, and all powerful . . . As the head and the body, as the husband and wife, so Christ and His saints are mutually concerned. They are rich or poor, stand and fall, live and die together. The husband conveys to the wife a title to what he has; as the wife holds of the husband, so it is between Christ and His church. They have nothing but through Him. Their whole tenure is in Him as the Head. Whatever is His is theirs. Whatever is theirs is His. His God is their God, His Father is their Father, His blood, His merits, His Spirit, His victories, all the spoils He has captured, all the revenue and income of His life and death – ALL IS THEIRS! He obeyed for them, He suffered for them, He lived for them, He died for them, He rose for them, He ascended for them, and He has set down on the right hand of God to act for them. This is that Jesus Who is given to us. This is He Who by covenant is made over to all His saints.

Richard Alleine

21
"THAT'S MY KING!"
WHO'S FAMOUS LIKE NO OTHER!

Jesus is more famous than all the famous ones in the universe!
He's the Famous of the famous!
Crowds flocked to Him from the north, south, east, and west!
Every kind of people worship Him as Lord, God, and Savior!
Young and old bow down to Him!
Rich and poor alike forsake all to follow Him!
Men and women from every political persuasion pursue His powerful, purifying presence!
All tribes, tongues, peoples, and nations will magnify His Name above all names!
Red and yellow, black and white, they are precious in His site, and they all adore Him above all!

That's my King! I wonder if He's famous in your heart today?!

The greatest book that's ever been written is all about Him!
His book is the bestseller of the universe!

CHRIST IS ALL!

Beginning with Moses and all the Prophets, He expounded in all the Scriptures the things concerning Himself!
The Scriptures, in which we have eternal life, testify of Him!
Moses wrote about Him!
All the prophets witness about Him!
The Father's final Word to us is Jesus Christ Himself!
The Father passionately purposed to make His Son famous!
The Father Who sent Him has Himself borne witness about Him!
The Father has sent Him to be the Savior of the world!
For God so loved the world, that He gave His only begotten Son, that whosoever believes in Him shall not perish but have everlasting life!

That's my King! Do you know Him?!

Jesus came to make an everlasting Name for Himself like no other Who has ever crossed the horizon of this world!
Everyone should honor the Son, just as they honor the Father!
Whoever has the Son has life; whoever does not have the Son does not have life!
He's the Bread of Life!
Everyone who comes to Him shall never hunger, and the one who believes in Him shall never thirst!
He's the Light of the world!
The one who follows Him shall not walk in darkness, but has the Light of life!
He's the Door!
If anyone enters by Him, they will be saved!
He's the Good Shepherd!
The Good Shepherd gave His life for the sheep!
He's the Resurrection and the Life!
He who believes in Him, though he may die, yet shall he live – forever!
He's the Way, the Truth, and the Life!
No one comes to the Father except through Him!

CHRIST IS ALL!

He is the vine and you are the branches, for without Him you can do nothing!

That's my King!

The Holy Spirit came to make Jesus even more famous and give Him glory!
The Apostles preached Jesus here, there, and everywhere!
Paul knew nothing among the Corinthians except Jesus Christ and Him crucified!
The best selling book that has every graced the face of this sinful earth is the B I B L E – and it's all about Him!
He's the Gospel, and He's the God-Man!
He's the LORD for Whom John the Baptizer prepared the way!
He's the mightiest of the mighty and none of us are worthy to untie His sandals!
He's God the Father's beloved Son with Whom the Father is well pleased!
He's the greater Adam and the greater Israel!
He's the Preacher of preachers Who taught with authority like no other who has ever been or who ever will be!
He says: "Follow Me!" and He's the Me of me's Who's magnetic like no other!
He's the Clean of cleans who touches skin diseased people, the diseases vanish, and everyone is clean!
He cast out demons – even devils obey Him and tremble at His presence!
He made the paralyzed walk!
He has authority to forgive sins – which only God can do!
No one ever saw anything like Him!
He's the Friend of friends to the sinner of sinners!
He's the Bridegroom of bridegroom's Who alone satisfies – and when He's around, you cannot fast!
But He's not around now in all His fullness, so we fast and long for His return!
He's the Lord of the Sabbath Who is God because God created the Sabbath, and He Himself is our true, everlasting Sabbath Rest!

CHRIST IS ALL!

Through His destruction on that cross and His resurrection from the dead we have life in His Name forevermore!

That's my King! That's my King!

Sinners, if you marry Him [Christ] all is yours.
All His riches are yours forever. If you are in debt even a
thousand talents, He has enough to pay all. All He asks is
your consent. Will you come to the King's supper?
Will you embrace Him, accept Him as your all? What do
you say? What answer shall I return to the
great King who sent me to you?

Gilbert Tennent

He is His beloved Son, the brightness of His glory, Whose
beauty God continually sees with infinite delight, without
ever being weary of beholding it. "I was daily His delight,
rejoicing always before Him" (Proverbs 8:30). And if the
angels and God Himself love Him so much above all, surely
children ought to love Him above all things in this world.

Everything that is lovely in God is in Him, and everything
that is or can be lovely in any man is in Him: for He is
man as well as God, and He is the holiest, meekest, most
humble, and in every way the most excellent man
that ever was. He is the delight of heaven.

There is nothing in heaven, that glorious world, that is
brighter and more amiable and lovely than Christ. And
this darling of heaven, by becoming man, became as a
plant or flower springing out of the earth. And He is the
most lovely flower that ever was seen in this world.

There is more good to be enjoyed in Him than in
everything or all things in this world. He is not only an
amiable, but an all-sufficient Good. There is enough in
Him to answer all our wants and satisfy all our desires.

Jonathan Edwards

22
"THAT'S MY KING!"
WHO'S THE GREATEST CARE,
THE MOST PRECIOUS RICHES, AND
THE MOST PASSIONATE DESIRE
IN ALL THE UNIVERSE!

He's the Care of all cares!
He's the one Care of this world Who will save you from caring about anything else!
In Him you can cast all your cares on Him because He cares for you!
He lavishes you with more love than any lover could ever duplicate, replicate, or that you could find in any Kate!
He tenderly cares for you like no mother could ever nurture, nurse, or nourish!
He pays attention to you like no poppa could ever provide, protect, or pastor!
He's got your back like no friend could ever help you, hold you, or handle all your problems!
He's the Big Brother Who takes up for you, took the blame for you, and tells you all you need to know!
He's the One Who says: "Peace be to you. I will care for all your desires!"

CHRIST IS ALL!

Your relationship to Him and His opinion of you should be the greatest care and concern of your life!
You ought to be careful to trust Him!
Careful to always listen to Him!
Careful to talk to Him!
Careful to love Him!
Careful to please Him!
Careful to obey Him!
Careful to delight in Him!
Careful to cherish Him!
Careful to treasure Him!
Careful to never offend Him!
And careful to go to Him for mercy every time you fail to be careful around Him in all those ways!

That's my King!

He most carefully cared for all those who would ever repent and believe in Him on that cross when He bore the careless sins of the world in His body on the tree!
He crushed all the curse ridden cares of His people when He conquered sin, death, and hell by rising from the grave!
He's so beautiful, loving, and satisfying that you constantly ought to have a love sickness for Him that takes your breath away!
He's the One Who, when you meet Him, you forget all the cares of the heartbreaks in your past as if they'd never happened!
He's the One Who, When you meet Him, songs rise up in your heart, the sky is bluer, the grass is greener, life is better, and all the cares of this world just fade away!
He perpetually ought to fill your stomach with more butterflies than ten thousand of your most cherished lovers!

That's my caring King! I wonder if you care about Him today?!

He's the Riches of all riches!

CHRIST IS ALL!

He's the most valuable, precious riches in all the universe
Who will never ever deceive you!
He only tells the truth!
Loves the truth!
Speaks the truth!
Lives the truth!
Shows the truth!
And He is the Truth incarnate – He is the Way, the Truth,
and the Life!
He's loaded!
He's wealthy!
He's filthy rich!
He's prosperous!
He's upscale!
He owns the cattle on a thousand hills!
He's more precious than thousands of pieces of gold and
silver!

That's my King!

He's the Pearl of great price!
He's the Treasure in the field worth selling everything for,
so that you can have Him!
He's worth more than all the riches and wealth of trillions
of worlds!
He made everything, owns everything, sustains everything,
and He is everything to those He came to save!
Though He was rich, yet for your sake He became poor,
suffered and died on that cross, and rose up from the
grave, so that you, by His poverty might become rich
forever and ever!
He's the riches of glory made known to God's vessels of
mercy!
He's the merciful riches of forgiveness for all manner of
poor, impoverished sinners!
He's the immeasurable riches of God's grace and kindness!
His riches are unsearchable, unknowable, unfathomable,
uncontainable, unstoppable, and unbelievable!

That's my Riches in glory!

CHRIST IS ALL!

Have you found your treasure in Him alone today?!

He's the Desire of all desires!
He's the Desire of the nations!
He's the Joy of all desiring!
He's good for food, a delight to the eyes, desirable to make us wise, and if you eat Him you'll be saved, safe, and satisfied forever![6]
His desire is for His people: only to bless them, only to care for them, and only to do them good for all eternity!
He alone can satisfy all your heart's desires!
He does all that He desires in heaven and on earth!
He's worthy to be sought after with the whole desires of our hearts, minds, souls, and strength!
He Himself is the Desire of every longing heart whether they know it or not!

That's my King! Do you know Him?!

His chief desire is to do His Father's will!
He's admirable!
He's ambitious!
He's appetizing!
He's attractive!
He's the Craze of all our covetous craving!
He's fascinating!
He's the all-consuming Preoccupation and insatiable Infatuation of all time!
He's the Living Water Who alone quenches all your thirsts!
He's the Bread of Life Who alone satisfies all your hungers!
He's captivating!
He's enthralling!
He's exhilarating!

---

6   John Piper used this phrase in the funeral sermon he gave for his father on March 9, 2007.
http://www.desiringgod.org/conference-messages/funeral-message-for-william-s-h-piper Accessed 21 JAN 2015.

CHRIST IS ALL!

He's propitiating – He satisfied the wrath of God against us on that cross and rose up from the grave, so that we could be reconciled to God and enjoy our hearts' greatest desire for all eternity!
All people, pleasures, positions, power, glory, girls, and gold that you have ever desired cannot compare with Him! He compels us to cry out with the Psalmist: "Whom have I in heaven but You! There is nothing on earth that I desire besides You!"
He's the Joy of joys, the Passion of passions, the Longing of longings, and the Delight of all delights!

That's my Desire! That's my King!

Jesus is all the world to me,
My life, my joy, my all!

Will Thompson

I say to the LORD, "You are my Lord;
I have no good apart from You."

Psalm 16:2

. . . strengthened and consoled by Jesus, the believer is not
afraid to die; no he is even willing to depart, for since he
has seen Jesus as the morning star, he longs to gaze upon
Him as the sun in his strength. Truly, the presence of
Jesus is all the heaven we desire. Jesus is at once: The
glory of our brightest days; the comfort of our nights.

Charles Spurgeon

23
"THAT'S MY KING!"
WHO'S THE GOOD-HEART OF
GOOD-HEARTS CAUSING THE
WORD OF GOD TO FLOURISH!

He hears the Word!
He hopes in the Word!
He humbles Himself under the Word!
He holds fast to the Word!
He hungers for the Word!
His heart stands in awe of the Word!
He believes the Word!
He fears the Word!
He keeps the Word!
He obeys the Word!
He pays careful attention to the Word!
He observes the Word!
He remembers the Word!
He does the Word!
He listens to the Word!
He stores up the Word in His Heart!
He trusts in the Word!
He rejoices in the Word!
He sings about the Word!

CHRIST IS ALL!

He trembles at the Word!

That's my King! I wonder if you know Him today?!

He receives the Word!
He considers the Word!
He abides in the Word!
He gives ear to the Word!
He receives the Word with much affliction and with the joy of the Holy Spirit!
He accepts the Word as the Word of God and not of men!
He's trained by the Word!
He follows the sound pattern of the Word!
He holds firm to the trustworthy Word!
He bears with the Word!
He walks in the Word!
He confirms the Word!
He knows the Word!
He gives Himself to the Word!
He studies the Word!
He understands the Word!
He turns back to the Word!
He greatly delights in the Word!
He meditates on the Word day and night!
He's refreshed by the Word!
He has the Word within His heart!
He beholds wondrous things in the Word!

That's my King!

He's taught by the Word!
He treasures the Word more than thousands of pieces of gold and silver!
He loves the Word!
He weeps because others do not obey the Word!
He magnifies the Word!
He fulfilled the Word!
He upholds the Word!
He submits to the Word!
He seeks out the Word!

CHRIST IS ALL!

He fixes His eyes on the Word!
He runs in the way of the Word!
He does not delay to keep the Word!
He learns the Word!
He loves the Word above gold, yea above fine gold!
He longs for the Word!
He keeps the Word as the apple of His eye!
He reveres the Word!
He finds the Word sweet to the taste, sweeter than honey
in the mouth!
He is the Word come in the flesh!
He taught, explained, parablized, preached, proclaimed,
and promiscuously provided the Word!
He was slain on that cross as the Word and to fulfill the
Word!
He rose up from the grave exactly according to the Word!
He bore more fruit than anyone who has ever crossed the
horizon of this world!
He's still bearing fruit right now all over the world as He
saves sinners from every tribe, tongue, people, and nation!
And He'll bear fruit for all eternity like no other heart ever
would, should, or could because His heart is so good!

That's my King! That's my King!

The highest of all God's commands is this, that we hold up before our eyes the image of His dear Son, our Lord Jesus Christ. Every day He should be our excellent mirror wherein we behold how much God loves us and how well, in His infinite goodness, He has cared for us in that He gave His dear Son for us . . . Contemplate Christ given for us. Then, God willing, you will feel better.

Martin Luther

Not I, but Christ be honored, loved, exalted,
Not I, but Christ be seen, be known and heard;
Not I, but Christ in every look and action,
Not I, but Christ in every thought and word.

Not I, but Christ to gently soothe in sorrow,
Not I, but Christ to wipe the falling tear;
Not I, but Christ to lift the weary burden,
Not I, but Christ to hush away all fear.

Christ, only Christ, no idle word e'er falling,
Christ, only Christ, no needless bustling sound;
Christ, only Christ, no self-important bearing,
Christ, only Christ, no trace of "I" be found.

Not I, but Christ my every need supplying,
Not I, but Christ my strength and health to be;
Christ, only Christ, for spirit, soul, and body,
Christ, only Christ, live then Thy life in me.

Christ, only Christ, ere long will fill my vision,
Glory excelling soon, full soon I'll see;
Christ, only Christ, my every wish fulfilling,
Christ, only Christ, my all in all to be.

Mrs. A. A. Whiddington

24
"THAT'S MY KING!"
WHO'S THE SECRET OF SECRETS
OF THE KINGDOM OF GOD!

He's the greatest Secret that has ever been concealed in this universe!
He's the Surprise of the ages!
He's the sure Secret!
He's the sovereign Secret!
He's the satisfying Secret!
All the secrets of wisdom are found in Him!
He's the revelation of the mystery that was kept secret since the beginning of the world but has now been made known!
He's the secret wisdom of another age, greater than all the rulers of this age, and destined to never pass away!
He's the secret place of refuge where we find safety from the wrath of God and confidence in His righteousness which surrounds us like rich robes of blood stained purity!
He's the Secret no eye has seen, nor ear heard, nor the heart of man imagined, that God has prepared for those who love Him!
He Himself is the Secret of knowing how to be content when you don't have anything!

CHRIST IS ALL!

And He's the Secret of contentment when you have
everything because you can do all things through Christ
Who strengthens you!
If you have Him and nothing else, then you have
everything and a whole lot more!
He's the Secret place of the Most High Who keeps you in
the shadow of the Almighty!
He's the Secret of God's will set forth at the fullness of time
to unite all things in Him, things in heaven and things on
earth!
He's the Secret Who was hidden from former generations
but Who has now been made known!

That's my King! Do you know Him!

He's the Secret Who brings together all races – Anglo,
African, Asian, Arab, Latino, Jew, and Gentile and
everyone else and makes them all one in Him!
He brings them all together, so that Christ is all and in all!
He's the Secret Who makes possible the broadcast of the
manifold wisdom of God to the rulers and authorities in
the heavenly places through the Church!
He's the Secret of all faithful marriages because they are all
to be little parables of Christ and His blood bought Bride –
the Church!
He's the Secret of the Gospel and its power to save and
change the hardest of hearts!
He's the riches of the glorious Secret that Christ is in you,
the hope of glory!
He's God's preeminent Secret in Whom is hidden all the
treasures of wisdom and knowledge!
He's the Secret worthy to be declared to every tribe,
tongue, people, and nation whether they want to hear
about Him or not!
He's the Secret to Whom every knee will bow someday,
willingly or unwillingly, and every tongue will confess that
He is Lord to the glory of God the Father!
He knows all the secrets of your heart and mind!
He heals all your secret hurts!
He fulfills and satisfies all your secret desires!

CHRIST IS ALL!

He's the only One Who can explain all the unexplainable secrets in your life with perfect precision, prudence, practicality, and piety!

That's my King!

He's the Secret of godliness!
He was manifested in the flesh!
He was justified by the Spirit!
He was seen by angels!
He's being proclaimed among the nations!
He's being believed on in the world!
He was taken up into glory!
He was the secret Suffering Servant Who was stricken, smitten by God and afflicted, wounded for our transgressions, and crushed by His Father on that cross, so that all those who ever repent and believe in Him might be saved!
He's the Secret of the empty tomb – He rose from the dead conquering sin, death, and hell, so that we might live in Him!
He's the Secret to the satisfaction you so long for that nothing in this world has, can, or ever will satisfy!
He's the out-of-this-world satisfying Secret Who alone satisfies all your deepest longings!
He Himself is the end of your search for the secret to satisfaction, serenity, and sanctification!
He's the Secret Who, when you find out about Him, compels you to sing, stomp your feet, celebrate, and shout about Him to others, so that they might know Him too!
He's the Secret that can't be kept, shouldn't be kept, and mustn't be kept but published, proclaimed, presented, and preached to all the world!
Go tell it on the mountain that Jesus Christ is Lord!

That's my King! That's my King!

O my Lord Jesus Christ, if I could be in heaven without Thee, it would be a hell; and if I could be in hell, and have Thee still, it would be a heaven to me, for Thou art all the heaven I want . . . Heaven and Christ are the same thing.

Samuel Rutherford

There will be little else we shall want of heaven besides Jesus Christ. He will be our bread, our food, our beauty, and our glorious dress. The atmosphere of heaven will be Christ; everything in heaven will be Christ-like: yes, Christ is the heaven of His people.

Charles Spurgeon

25
"THAT'S MY KING!"
WHO IS HEAVEN ITSELF!

He's not abrasive or irritating![7]
He's not agitating or hurtful!
He's not harmful or hateful!
He's not upsetting or unkind!
He's not sad, bad, or mad!
He's not harsh, impatient, ungrateful, or unworthy!
He's not weak or sick or broken or foolish!
Nothing in Him is deformed, degenerate, depraved, or disgusting!
He's not polluted, pathetic, poor, or putrid!
He's not dark, dismal, dismaying, or degrading!
Nothing in Him is blameworthy, blemished, blasphemous, or blighted!
He's not faulty, faithless, frail, or fading!
He's not grotesque or grievous, hideous, or insidious!

---

7   This list of adjectives was taken from Sam Storms' sermon,
     "Joy's Eternal Increase: Edwards On The Beauty Of
     Heaven," 2003 Desiring God National Conference:
     http://www.desiringgod.org/conference-messages/joys-
     eternal-increase-edwards-on-the-beauty-of-heaven
     Accessed 01 JAN 2015.

CHRIST IS ALL!

He's not illicit or illegal, lascivious or lustful!
He's not marred or mutilated, misaligned or misinformed!
He's not nasty or naughty, offensive or odious!
Nothing in Him is rancid or rude, soiled or spoiled, tawdry
or tainted, tasteless or tempting!
He's not vile or vicious, wasteful or wanton!
He's none of it!
And He's none of it, so that hell deserving sinners, like you
and me, might enjoy Him forever!

That's my King! I wonder if you know Him today?!

He's the glory of heaven!
He's the grandeur of heaven!
He's the beauty of heaven!
He's the brightness of heaven!
He's the purity of heaven!
He's the perfection of heaven!
He's the splendor of heaven!
He's the satisfaction of heaven!
He's the sweetness of heaven!
He's the salvation of heaven!
He's the majesty of heaven!
He's the adorability of heaven!
He's the affection of heaven!
He's the brilliance of heaven!
He's the bounty of heaven!
He's the delight of heaven!
He's the deliciousness of heaven!

That's my King!

He's the delectableness of heaven!
He's the dazzle of heaven!
He's the elegance of heaven!
He's the excitement of heaven!
He's the fascination of heaven!
He's the fruitfulness of heaven!
He's the grandness of heaven!
He's the graciousness of heaven!

CHRIST IS ALL!

He's the goodness of heaven!
He's the happiness of heaven!
He's the holiness of heaven!
He's the health of heaven!
He's the wholeness of heaven!
He's the joy of heaven!
He's the jubilance of heaven!
He's the loveliness of heaven!
He's the lusciousness of heaven!

That's my King! Do you know Him?!

He's the majesty of heaven!
He's the marvel of heaven!
He's the opulence of heaven!
He's the overwhelmingness of heaven!
He's the radiance of heaven!
He's the resplendence of heaven!
He's the splendidness of heaven!
He's the sublimeness of heaven!
He's the sweetness of heaven!
He's the savor of heaven!
He's the tenderness of heaven!
He's the tastefulness of heaven!
He's the unity of heaven!
He's euphoria of heaven!
He's the ecstasy of heaven!
He's all of this and more – He's the Lamb of God Who
takes away the sin of the world!
He's all of this, so that hell deserving sinners, like you and
me, might enjoy Him in all His fulness forevermore!

That's my King! That's my King!

It is so sweet to look at the Crucified One again, and say, "I have nothing but Thee, my Lord, no confidence but Thee. If You are not accepted as my substitute then I must perish. If God's appointed Savior is not enough then I have no other. But I know You are the Father's well-beloved, and I am accepted in Thee. You are all I have or want."

Charles Spurgeon

Christ our Lord alone is the One Who is, gives, and performs for us everything which we can desire for our true advantage, happiness, and honor . . . all gain, all enjoyment, all honor apart from Christ is poison and death, but . . . in Christ all loss is true and eternal gain, joy, and honor . . . through the holy Gospel of Christ people are well instructed and reminded to seek everything in Christ our Lord alone and be satisfied with all things in Him . . . we have all our joy, comfort, and confidence in Him, Christ our Lord. If we really love Christ, He is everything to us . . .

Martin Bucer

26
"THAT'S MY KING!"
WHO GIVES FREEDOM
LIKE NO OTHER!

He's freedom come in the flesh!
He's the freest of all beings in the universe!
He's the freest of the free!
He's the free Gift of heaven!
He's the free Gift of God!
He's the free Gift of grace!
He's the free Gift of righteousness!
He's the free Gift of holiness!
He's the free Gift of redemption!
He's the free Gift of glory!
He sought freedom!
He bought freedom!
He brought freedom!
He wrought freedom!
He fought for freedom!
He won this freedom when He died on that cross and rose up from the grave!
He freed Himself from the chains of death and conquered sin, death, and Satan, so that all those who repent and believe in Him might be free and saved forever!

CHRIST IS ALL!

That's my King! I wonder if you have freedom in Him
today?!

He's the Son Who sets us free, so that we might be free
indeed!
He frees from sin!
He frees from hell!
He frees from death!
He frees from boredom!
He frees from cares!
He frees from worries!
He frees from fear!
He frees from bondage!
He frees from slavery!
He frees from all idolatry!
He sets us free from the love of money!
He frees from adultery, fornication, pornography, and all
sexual immorality!
He frees from lying, stealing, rebellion, murder, and all
coveting!
He frees from lovelessness, hypocrisy, selfishness, and all
sin – which is God-murder!
He frees from the wrath of God!
He loves us, and He freed us from our sins by His blood!

That's my King!

He frees from all false religions that lead to hell – Islam,
Hinduism, Judaism, Buddhism, and all the other "isms" in
this world!
He sets us free from the law of sin and death, so that we
might be married to Him in wedded bliss forever!
He frees from all addictions, afflictions, and
contradictions!
He frees from all pain, sorrow, and tears!
He frees us from the cares of this world, the deceitfulness
of riches, and the desires for other things!
He frees us from the deepest longings of our hearts because
He satisfies them all with Himself!
For freedom He has set us free!

CHRIST IS ALL!

He ushered in the new creation and will finally set it free
from its bondage to decay, so that it might obtain the
freedom of the glory of the children of God!
He's the Lord Who is the Spirit, and where the Spirit of the
Lord is, there is freedom indeed!
He's the Brave-Heart of brave-hearts and the Mercy-Heart
of mercy-hearts all in One, so that in Him we can cry
"Freedom!" and "Mercy!" all at the same time!

That's my King! Do you know Him?!

He frees from disabilities!
He frees from barrenness!
He frees from cancer!
He frees from heart disease!
He frees from leprosy!
He frees from old age!
He frees you from everything you don't want, wish you
never had, and never want to remember!
He frees you from your past, present, and future that you
long to be erased from your memory forever!
He frees you to enjoy Him as the greatest Treasure of your
life forever!
He frees you to delight in Him above all things!
He frees you to glorify Him and enjoy Him forever!
He frees you to love His law and commandments more
than thousands of pieces of gold and silver!
He frees you to deny yourself, pick up your cross daily, and
follow Him!
He frees you to hate everything you most cherish in this life
compared to the love you have for Him!
He frees you to love with an incomprehensible love the
most lovely Object that has ever crossed the horizon of this
world!

That's my King!

He can let freedom ring from the brothels in Thailand and
India!

CHRIST IS ALL!

He can let freedom ring in the hearts of drug addicts and dealers in the inner cities of America!
He can let freedom ring in the hearts of the 143 million orphans in this world!
He can let freedom ring in the hearts of the 18,000 children who starve to death each day!
He can let freedom ring in the hearts of the thousands of fathers and mothers who weep over their starving children daily!
He can let freedom ring in the hearts of the 27 million people enslaved around the world today!
He can let freedom ring among all pimps, slave owners, and sex offenders!
He can let freedom ring in the hearts of the vilest of the vile!
He can let freedom ring in the hearts of racist Klansmen in Mississippi!
He can let freedom ring in the hardest hearted Al-Qaeda and ISIS terrorists!
He can let freedom ring from the most unbeatable, unbreakable, unrelenting, addictive habitual sin ever experienced in this universe!
He can let freedom ring in the hearts of church goers who are so proud, cold, and dead that He warns them that He'll vomit them out of His mouth!
He can let freedom ring in the pastor who's more proud of his poetry about Christ than He is of Christ Himself!
He can let freedom ring in the 7,000 unreached people groups in this world who have never heard His name!

Will you go and tell them about our King today?!

Will you go and live in the freedom of Christ today?!

He is worthy!

That's my King! That's my King!

I would purpose that the subject of the ministry in this house, as long as this platform shall stand, and as long as this house shall be frequented by worshipers, shall be the person of JESUS CHRIST. I am never ashamed to avow myself a Calvinist; I do not hesitate to take the name of Baptist; But if I am asked what is my creed, I reply – It is JESUS CHRIST. My venerated predecessor, Dr. Gill, has left a body of divinity, admirable and excellent in its way; but the body of divinity to which I would pin and bind myself forever, God helping me, is not his system or any other human treatise; but CHRIST JESUS, Who is the sum and substance of the gospel, Who is in Himself all theology, the incarnation of every precious truth, the all-glorious personal embodiment of the way, the truth, and the life.

Charles Spurgeon's reported first words at the Metropolitan Tabernacle in London

27
"THAT'S MY KING!"
WHO'S THE LION AND THE LAMB
ALL AT THE SAME TIME!

He's the Lion of the tribe of Judah Who roars and all the
rulers of the world hush silent![8]
And at the same time He's the Lamb slain for the sins of
the whole world!
There is in Him an admirable conjunction of diverse
excellencies like no other being this world has ever seen!
He excels in strength and majesty, and also in meekness
and patience!
In Him do meet together infinite highness and infinite
condescension!
He's God Himself!
He's infinitely great and high above all!
He's higher than all the kings of the earth!

---

8   Content for this chapter is taken from Jonathan Edwards'
     sermon, "The Admirable Conjunction of Diverse Excellencies
     in Christ Jesus."
     http://www.monergism.com/thethreshold/articles/onsite/a
     dmirable.html Accessed 01 JAN 2015.

CHRIST IS ALL!

He's higher than the heavens, and higher than the highest angels of heaven!
He's so great that all men, kings, potentates, princes, and presidents are as worms of the dust before Him!
Before Him all the nations are as drops in a bucket!
The angels themselves are as nothing before Him!
He's so high that He's infinitely above any need of His creatures!
He's the Creator and great Possessor of heaven and earth!
He's sovereign Lord of all!
He rules over the whole universe and does whatever He pleases!
His knowledge is without bound!
His wisdom is perfect!
His power is infinite, and none can resist Him!
His riches are immense and inexhaustible!
His majesty is infinitely amazing!

That's my King! I wonder if you know Him today?!

And yet He's One of infinite condescension!
He takes notice of the lowest of the low and cares for them with the most tender love!
He condescends to help the poorest creatures of this universe!
He loves the despised!
He accepts the rejected!
He takes notice of beggars!
He cares for the little children that no one else wants to touch!
He condescends to take gracious, merciful notice of the most unworthy, sinful creatures who deserve nothing good but only deserve suffering and hell!
He condescends to become the friend of sinners!
He becomes the companion of the wicked and unites His soul to the ungodly in spiritual marriage!
He became like one of us, so that He could become one with us!
He exposed Himself to shame and spitting!

CHRIST IS ALL!

He endured the most horrific death that has ever crossed the horizon of this world!
He humbled Himself like no other has ever humbled himself in the history of this world!
And He did all this for sinners like you and me – the low, the despicable, the unworthy!

That's my King!

In Him do meet together infinite justice and infinite grace!
He's infinitely holy and just!
He hates sin like no other!
He'll execute punishment for all sin!
He's the Judge of all the earth!
He's the infinitely just Judge over all!
He won't at all acquit the wicked or by any means clear the guilty!
Yet He's infinitely gracious and merciful at the same time!
His justice is so strict with respect to all sin, and every breach of the law!
Yet He has grace sufficient for every sinner – even the chief of sinners!
He can bestow the greatest good upon the greatest of sinners!
He does good to sinners!
He works all things for good on behalf of sinners!
He suffered for sinners!
He suffered the most extreme death for sinners!
He suffered the infinite wrath of God on the cross, so that sinners might be saved!

That's my King! Do you know Him?!

In Him do meet together infinite glory and lowest humility!
Infinite glory and the virtue of humility meet in no other person but Christ!
He's both fully God and fully man!
He must be honored just as the Father is honored!
He must be worshiped, adored, and bowed down to!
Yet He's the lowest of all in humility at the same time!

CHRIST IS ALL!

He's the humblest of the humble!
He was perfectly content with His lowly outward circumstances!
He lived in poverty, was born into a poor family, and was born in the feeding trough of a cow!
He washed His disciples' feet!
He took the form of a servant!
He humbled Himself to the point of death, even death on that cross!

That's my King!

In Him meet together infinite majesty and transcendent meekness!
These meet together in no other person but Christ!
Being both God and man, He possesses infinite majesty and superlative meekness!
He's mighty, riding on the heavens and His excellency on the sky!
He's awesome out of His holy places!
He's mightier than the noise of many waters, yes, than the mighty waves of the sea: before Whom a fire goes, and burns up His enemies round about!
At His presence the earth quakes, and the hills melt!
He sits on the circle of the earth, and all the inhabitants of the earth are as grasshoppers!
He rebukes the sea and makes it dry and dries up the rivers!
His eyes are as a flame of fire!
From His presence and from the glory of His power the wicked shall be punished with everlasting destruction!
He's the blessed and only Potentate, the King of kings, and Lord of lords!
He has heaven for His throne and the earth for His footstool!
He's the high and lofty One who inhabits eternity!

That's my King!

His kingdom is an everlasting kingdom, and of His
dominion there is no end!
And yet He was also the most marvelous instance of
meekness and humble quietness of spirit that ever was or
ever will be!
He's the King that came, meek, and sitting on a donkey!
He's meek and lowly in heart!
There never was such an example of meek behavior seen
on earth in the face of all manner of torments, reproaches,
and evils!
He loved His enemies!
When He was reviled He reviled not in return!
He had the most wonderful spirit of forgiveness!
He prayed for His enemies with fervent, effectual prayers!
Against His mocking enemies He opened not His mouth
but went as a lamb to the slaughter!
He's the Lion in majesty and the Lamb in meekness!

That's my King! Do you know Him?!

In Him meet together the deepest reverence towards God
and equality with God!
He always appeared full of holy reverence towards the
Father!
He paid the most reverential worship to Him, praying to
Him with postures of reverence!
His person was in all respects equal to the person of the
Father!
God the Father has no attribute or perfection that the Son
has not, in equal degree, and equal in glory!
These things meet in no other person but Jesus Christ!
There are conjoined in Him infinite worthiness of good,
and the greatest patience under sufferings of evil!
He was perfectly innocent, and deserved no suffering!
He deserved nothing from God by any guilt of His own,
and He deserved no bad from any men!
He was not only harmless and undeserving of suffering,
but He was infinitely worthy of all good!

CHRIST IS ALL!

He's worthy of the infinite love of the Father, worthy of infinite and eternal happiness, and infinitely worthy of all possible esteem, love, and service from all men!
And yet He was perfectly patient under the greatest sufferings that ever were endured in this world!
He endured the cross, despising the shame!
He suffered not from His Father for His faults, but for our faults!
He suffered from men not for His faults but for those things on account of which He was infinitely worthy of their love and honor, which made His patience the more wonderful and the more glorious!
He did no sin, neither was guile found in His mouth: Who when He was reviled, reviled not in return, when He suffered, He threatened not, but committed Himself to Him that judges righteously: Who His own self bore our sins in His own body on the tree, that we being dead to sin, should live unto righteousness: by Whose stripes you have been healed!
There is no such conjunction of innocence, worthiness, and patience under sufferings, as in the person of Christ!

That's my King!

In Him are conjoined an exceeding spirit of obedience with supreme dominion over heaven and earth!
Christ is the Lord of all things in two respects: He is God-Man and Mediator!
His dominion is appointed and given Him of the Father!
But He's Lord of all things in another respect, namely, as He is God; and so He is by natural right the Lord of all and supreme over all as much as the Father!
He has dominion over the world, not by delegation, but in His own right!
He is not under God but to all intents and purposes supreme God!
And yet in the same Person is found the greatest spirit of obedience to the commands and laws of God that ever was in the universe!
As the Father gave Him commandment, even so He did!

CHRIST IS ALL!

He kept His Father's commandments and dwelt in His love!
Never has anyone received commands from God of such difficulty, and that were so great a trial of obedience, as Jesus Christ!
And He was thoroughly obedient in all of these commands of God!
Never was there such an instance of obedience in man or angel as this, though He was at the same time supreme Lord of both angels and men!

That's my King! Do you know Him?!

In Him are conjoined absolute sovereignty and perfect submission!
This is another unparalleled conjunction!
Christ, as He is God, is the absolute sovereign of the world, the sovereign disposer of all events! The decrees of God are all His sovereign decrees!
The work of creation and all God's works of providence are His sovereign works!
It is He Who works all things according to the counsel of His own will!
By Him, and through Him, and to Him, are all things!
But yet Christ was the most wonderful instance of submission that has ever appeared in the world!
He was absolutely and perfectly submissive when He had a near and immediate prospect of His terrible sufferings, and the dreadful cup that He was to drink!
The idea and expectation of this made His soul exceeding sorrowful even unto death and put Him into such an agony that His sweat was as it were great drops or clots of blood, falling down to the ground!
But in such circumstances He was wholly submissive to the will of God!
In Him do meet together self-sufficiency and an entire trust and reliance on God!
He's the divine person, self-sufficient, and standing in need of nothing!
All creatures are dependent on Him!

CHRIST IS ALL!

He's dependent on none, but is absolutely independent!
His proceeding from the Father, in His eternal generation,
argues no proper dependence on the will of the Father; for
that proceeding was natural and necessary!
But yet He entirely trusted in God!

That's my King! That's my King!

Delight yourself in the LORD, and He will
give you the desires of your heart.

Psalm 37:4

God is most glorified in us
when we are most satisfied in Him.

John Piper

The end [goal] of the creation of God was to provide a
spouse for His Son Jesus Christ that might enjoy Him and
on whom He might pour forth His love. And the end of all
things in providence are to make way for the exceeding
expressions of Christ's love to His spouse and for her
exceeding close and intimate union with, and high and
glorious enjoyment of Him and to bring this to pass. And
therefore the last thing and the issue of all things is the
marriage of the Lamb. And the wedding day is the last day,
the day of judgment, or rather that will be the beginning of
it. The wedding feast is eternal; and the love and joys, the
songs, entertainments and glories of the wedding never
will be ended. It will be an everlasting wedding day.

Jonathan Edwards

28
"THAT'S MY KING!"
WHO'S THE OLYMPIAN
OF ALL OLYMPIANS!

This was written during the 2012 Summer Olympics held in London.

Olympian: Majestic in manner; Surpassing all others in scope and effect . . . One who is superior to all others.[9]

Oh boy this will preach . . .

He's the greatest Olympian of all time, and no one can ever compare with Him!
He's the majestic of the majestic!
He's more majestic in manner than all the manners that have ever been produced, introduced, or reproduced!

---

9   Copyright © 2011 by Houghton Mifflin Harcourt Publishing Company. Adapted and reproduced by permission from The American Heritage Dictionary of the English Language, Fifth Edition. http://www.thefreedictionary.com/Olympian, Accessed 13 DEC 2015.

CHRIST IS ALL!

He surpasses all others in scope and effect like this world has never seen!
The scope of His influence on this universe is incomparable!
The far reaching effects of His life, death, and resurrection cannot be contained, chained, or fully explained!
He's the One Who's superior to all others including brothers, mothers, and all anothers!
He's in a class by Himself!
He stands on a podium made by Himself, upheld by Himself, and all by Himself!
To know Him and to be known by Him is worth more than all the gold, silver, and bronze of 10 trillion universes!
His Word is worth more than thousands of pieces of gold and silver!
He's the priceless golden treasure of this universe Who alone can satisfy your soul!

That's my King! I wonder if you know Him today?!

He ran the only perfect race that's ever been run in the history of this world!
He ran the fastest race, the smartest race, the longest race, and the best race all at the same time!
His life was full of perfect "10's" in all areas – any time, every time, all the time!
He's the only one Who disciplined His body perfectly with perpetually passionate power to produce the purest personal performance of any person Who has ever crossed the horizon of this world!
He's dedicated!
He's determined!
He's focused!
He's passionate!
He's strong!
He's gifted!
He's talented!
He's powerful!
He's skilled!
He's precise!

CHRIST IS ALL!

He's undaunted!
He's relentless!
He's unbreakable!
He's unstoppable!
He's unbeatable!
All He does is win!

That's my King!

He created Michael Phelps; gave him all his gifts, talents,
abilities, and work ethic; caused him to be born in an
environment where those gifts could all be developed; gave
him all the opportunities he was given to succeed; gave him
all his wins and medals; and upholds him and everything
else in this universe by the Word of His power!
He's Gabby Douglas's Creator, Lord, and Master; He made
her hair and it looks great just like it is, and only through
His grace, love, and mercy can she flip, cartwheel, and
handstand for the glory of God!
He made Usain Bolt's legs; He made Usain Bolt fast; He
gives Usain Bolt life and breath and everything; and He
deserves all the glory for everything Usain Bolt does!
May it be that when Usain Bolt runs He feels King Jesus'
pleasure!
He's the Dream Team of dream teams, and He's the
deepest dream of every human heart whether they know it
or not!
There's no one like Him!
He wins everything by just as many points as He pleases!
When you see these athletes perform, may their dedication,
talent, power, glory, and beauty always point you to their
Creator and Sustainer Who gave them all these gifts and
Who is infinitely more powerful, glorious, and beautiful
than all of them combined by an infinite distance!

That's my King! Do you know Him?!

He's the Underdog of underdogs and the Champion of
champions all at the same time!

He won it all through defeat, and through defeat He won it all!

He took upon Himself all your loses, failures, defeats, and rejections, so that you might never lose, fail, be defeated, or be rejected again!

He took upon Himself all your laziness, weakness, lack of dedication, sin, and ugliness, so that you might be revived, strengthened, committed, forgiven, and beautiful in God's eyes – covered with the very righteousness of Jesus Christ Himself!

He lost everything that matters most on that cross, so that He might win it all back and a whole lot more!

He was absolutely crushed in defeat, so that He and all His blood bought people might never be defeated again!

God raised Him up from the grave, victorious over sin, death, and Satan for all time, so that by faith in Him you might win the victory too!

He ran to obtain the prize, and He did obtain it, and He Himself is the greatest Prize, all at the same time!

He exercised self-control in all things like no other!

He did not run to receive a perishable wreath, but an imperishable one, and He did receive it, so that we might go and do likewise!

Therefore, let us also lay aside every weight and sin which clings so closely!

Let us run with endurance the race that is set before us by looking to Jesus, the Founder and Perfecter of our faith!

For the joy that was set before Him, He endured the cross, despising the shame, and is seated at the right hand of the throne of God!

Consider Him Who endured from sinners such hostility against Himself, so that you may not grow weary or fainthearted!

That's my King! That's my King!

Whom have I in heaven but Thee?

Psalm 73:25

David declares that he desires nothing, either in heaven or in earth, except God alone, and that without God, all other objects which usually draw the hearts of men towards them were unattractive to him. And, undoubtedly, God then obtains from us the glory to which He is entitled, when, instead of being carried first to one object, and then to another, we hold exclusively by Him, being satisfied with Him alone. If we give the smallest portion of our affections to the creatures, we in so far defraud God of the honor which belongs to Him. And yet nothing has been more common in all ages than this sacrilege, and it prevails too much at the present day. How small is the number of those who keep their affections fixed on God alone!

John Calvin

29
"THAT'S MY KING!"
WHO'S THE TEACHER, OFFENDER,
AND HUMAN SOUL MENDER!

He's the truth Defender
Who calls for surrender
The disciple Maker and Sender
The all races Blender
The forever evil Suspender
The Teacher Who's tender and gloriously arrayed in
unimaginable splendor!

His true disciples must trust and follow Him
Otherwise their claims to love Him are just a whim
And their future's only dim and grim
So don't just sing a hymn
But delight in Him
To find joy filled to the brim
And in Him, your ocean of pleasure, you can forever swim!

CHRIST IS ALL!

In Nazareth He met rejection
They showed Him no affection
To His person and work they gave objection
This made clear their sinful infection
Because He's the ultimate display of all perfection
And He forever proved this through His death and
resurrection
Giving glory to His Father of Whom He's the exact
reflection
And forever cleansing His people from all imperfection!

He's the Teacher of teachers
Who's also the Prince of preachers
He powerfully rules over every creature
And by an infinite distance He's the universe's most
beautiful feature!

That's my King! I wonder if you know Him today?!

When they heard Him they were dazed and amazed
But their hearts were left unfazed
When they should have bowed down and praised
This God-Man Who would soon die and be raised!

His hometown He offended
When instead they should have comprehended
His divine character and beauty truly splendid
On that cross He was expended
And His life was ended
But then forever extended
Just as His Father always intended!

He's the greatest Prophet without honor
Yet there's no one fonder
He's the only one to conquer
All for the glory of His Father!

CHRIST IS ALL!

Faith in Him they truly lacked
Though reasons to trust Him couldn't be more packed,
stacked, or better backed
But still He'd interact
Until finally they attacked
But through His death He had the greatest impact!

So won't you trust Him now
To delight in Him He'll show you how
To be His co-heir He'll allow
To you the whole world He'll endow
He'll mend your soul and with joy lift your brow
To Him alone you'll bow
And enjoy in His presence the everlasting wow!

That's my King! That's my King!

The saints' delight is in Christ: He is their joy, their crown, their rejoicing, their life, food, health, strength, desire, righteousness, salvation, blessedness: without Him they have nothing; in Him they shall find all things. "God forbid that I should glory, save in the cross of our Lord Jesus Christ" (Gal. 6:14). He has, from the foundation of the world, been the hope, expectation, desire, and delight of all believers.

John Owen

I do desire for my fellow Christians and for myself, that more and more the great object of our thoughts, motives, and acts may be "Jesus only." I believe that whenever our religion is most vital, it is most full of Christ. Moreover, when it is most practical, downright, and common sense, it always gets nearest to Jesus. I can bear witness that whenever I am in deeps of sorrow, nothing will do for me but "Jesus only." . . . I find if I want to labor much, I must live on Jesus only; if I desire to suffer patiently, I must feed on Jesus only; if I wish to wrestle with God successfully, I must plead Jesus only; if I aspire to conquer sin, I must use the blood of Jesus only; if I pant to learn the mysteries of heaven, I must seek the teachings of Jesus only. I believe that any thing which we add to Christ lowers our position, and that the more elevated our soul becomes, the more nearly like what it is to be when it shall enter into the religion of the perfect, the more completely every thing else will sink, die out, and Jesus, Jesus, Jesus only, will be First and Last, and midst and without end, the Alpha and Omega of every thought of head and pulse of heart.

Charles Spurgeon

30
"THAT'S MY KING!"
WHOSE NAME DEMANDS FAME
WHICH WE MUST DIE TO PROCLAIM!

He so lived and so spoke that His name became known
Since then His fame has continually grown
For He must be honored just as His Father on the throne
He humbled Himself to the point of death all alone
He absorbed God's wrath for sin to atone
Yet He's alive forevermore – from the grave He's flown
All over the world His Gospel will be sown
Calling sinners to Himself and making them His very own!

He's the God-Man with incomparable fame
He came to heal the lame
And all those afflicted with shame
He's the Lion of God Who's good but not tame
His followers must aim to proclaim
The wonderful excellencies of His great, matchless name!

Holiness and righteousness are His demand
Life with Him is not bland
But abundantly grand
His love and beauty you can't withstand

CHRIST IS ALL!

Your life couldn't be better planned
So reach out by faith and take His hand
Fight for holiness and take your stand
Striving to obey His every command
So that one day you'll enter the promised land!

About Him we must speak
He's utterly unique
Don't worry about your technique
Or your voice mild and weak
But only seek
With a heart that's meek
To tell of a future so bleak
Without the glorious salvation He purchased during holy
week!

That's my King! I wonder if you know Him today?!

When Jesus calls you, He calls you to death
But in the process He'll take away your breath
And ultimately give you a high better than meth!

Some like John will die as a martyr
Life on earth couldn't be harder
But God's truth over life they do prefer
Threats of suffering and death will not deter
For Christ's love in their hearts will captivate and stir
A great reward God will eternally confer!

Others will die smaller deaths day by day
Death to self and to all the "good things" He seems to delay
The idols of the heart we're called to slay
Christ must be first, it's the only way
So your number one lover don't betray
But cry "Christ is all!" and His worth display!

CHRIST IS ALL!

Don't sigh and ask Him why
Just plead and cry
For Him to help you die
And fix your eye
On His everlasting supply
Full of love, joy, and mercy that will never run dry
Him you'll never deny
But to His everlasting arms you'll fly
And with His infinite beauty He'll forever satisfy!

What you so long for is only a whore
It's stealing your love and only wants more
It, you must abhor and deplore
Against it make war I implore
So that you might be set free to soar
Up from the floor and fly to explore
The King's great beauty galore
Where there's fullness of joy and pleasures forevermore!

That's my King! That's my King!

This I know: that in the immediate beholding of the person of Christ we shall see a glory in it a thousand times above what here we can conceive. The excellencies of infinite wisdom, love, and power therein, will be continually before us.

And all the glories of the Person of Christ which we have before weakly and faintly inquired into, will be in our sight forevermore. Hence the ground and cause of our blessedness is that "we shall ever be with the Lord," (1 Thess. 4:17), as He Himself prays, "that we may be with Him where He is, to behold His glory" (John 17:24).

We cannot perfectly behold it until we are with Him where He is. There our sight of Him will be direct, intuitive, and constant. There is a glory, there will be so, subjectively in us in the beholding of this glory of Christ, which is at present incomprehensible.

For it doth not yet appear what we ourselves shall be (cf. 1 John 3:2). Who can declare what a glory it will be in us to behold this glory of Christ? And how excellent, then, is that glory of Christ itself? This immediate sight of Christ is that which all the saints of God in this life do breathe and pant after.

John Owen

31
"THAT'S MY KING!"
WHO'S THE PROPHET, GOOD SHEPHERD, AND PROVIDER WHOSE STRONG ARMS OF MERCY CAN'T BE OPENED WIDER!

He had compassion on the crowd
Though they were proud
And without a leader poorly endowed
He taught them truth out loud
While they sat under the cloud
Until their stomachs growled
And with His power to provide He wowed the crowd
And gave them more food than their appetites allowed
He's God come down – they should have bowed
And to Him alone all allegiance avowed!

People came to Him from every place
Though He had no desirable face
He and His disciples couldn't hide from the chase
Or slow down their pace
And they had no personal space
But He kept showing love and grace
That would eventually spread to every race!

CHRIST IS ALL!

He's the Prophet like Moses Who was to come
Though they didn't know where He came from
He was spit upon, killed, and treated like scum
But He rose from the grave, lifting up from the slum
Of all beauty and good He's the infinite sum!

He's the Good Shepherd Who had to die
"Is there another way?!" was His holy cry
Forsaken on the cross He asked His Father why
He obeyed the Divine will and did comply without a sigh
He glorified the Most High
And kept His eye fixed on the joy to come by and by
To win for us mercy of endless supply
If on Him alone we'll only rely
So what's your reply
To His arms may you forever fly!

That's my King! I wonder if you know Him today?!

He's the Bread of Life
Who died for His wife
In order to finally end all strife!

He's the Bread that was broken
An incomparable Token
God's final Word spoken
From the dead He's awoken
To save His chosen
Restore their emotion
And win their devotion
As He makes a way open
To enjoy His bottomless love-mercy ocean!

He's the Bread Who came down to wipe away the Father's
frown
He won the crown for His Father's renown
He's the most precious noun of any town around
In His glory and beauty we can drown
When sin increases His grace will abound
He's the Master of the lost and found

CHRIST IS ALL!

He's like the heavenly hound
He'll chase you down
He died but rose up from the ground
So His mercy would surround
His enemies confound
And His people forever astound
With His glory unspeakably profound!

All your needs He will provide
Since He died to make you His bride
He'll kill your pride and be your guide
He's forever and always on your side
So put all sin aside and in Him abide
Even though your tempted and tried
His arms are open wide
So run to Him – in His mercy hide
And spread His Gospel worldwide
So you can praise His name in heaven with all nations side
by side!

He satisfies the desire of every living thing
Of all pleasure and joy He's the everlasting Spring
He can't help but make you sing
Because of all the delight He'll bring
So turn from every other empty fling
And flee to Him and cling
Because He's the only all satisfying King!

That's my King! That's my King!

These inward trials I employ
from self and pride to set thee free
and break thy schemes of earthly joy
that thou may'st find thy all in me.

John Newton

Here perfect bliss can ne'er be found,
the honey's mix'd with gall;
Midst changing scenes and dying friends,
be Thou my all in all.

Benjamin Beddome

I hear the Savior say, Thy strength indeed is small,
Child of weakness, watch and pray,
Find in Me thine all in all.

Elvina Hall

Be still, my soul: thy Jesus can repay
from His own fullness all He takes away.

Katharina A. von Schlegel

32
"THAT'S MY KING!"
WHO'S THE CENTER
OF ALL THANKSGIVING
AS THE GOD OF THE LIVING
THROUGH HIS MERCIFUL
FORGIVING!

As you enjoy your thanksgiving food
Don't forget the Seed and serpent feud
When Adam fell the war ensued
Because the serpent crass and crude
So bad the lying devil shrewd
God's Word to Eve and Adam skewed
Then in the world all evil brewed
From garden bliss He did exclude
All sinners with their attitude
But God sent Christ to change the mood
In this dark world Light would intrude
His whole life worthiness accrued
And at His death He's stripped and nude
And treated as unwanted lewd
He won the war – it did conclude
Death's jaws He would finally elude

CHRIST IS ALL!

By evil He won't be subdued
This the whole world He renewed
And in your sin and hatred rude
By mercy He in love pursued
So you in heaven He'd include
Through faith in Him His beauty's viewed!

That's my King!

Now He's the center of all your praise
All His good gifts are merely rays
That point us back to the Ancient of Days
He's the Sun that burns our idol haze
And sets our hearts for Him ablaze
He blesses with gifts in manifold ways
But to the Source our eyes must raise
With Him alone allegiance stays
His grace and glory all amaze!

In every delight you've ever desired
Christ is the joy you most truly admired
Every good gift from Him is inspired
For lasting deep joy He's required
With the Father and Spirit He's conspired
To ensure fullness of joy in Him is acquired!

Be thankful that He saved from hell
Now with your soul it all is well
In His house forever you'll dwell
All your sin He'll finally expel
In righteousness you'll truly excel
So from the mountain go and yell
And everyone His Gospel tell
For His great love this will compel!

That's my King! Do you know Him?!

Be thankful He's a sovereign King
Elect He chose under His wing
Totally depraved – a sinful spring

CHRIST IS ALL!

He died for them to make them clean
Irresistibly to God He'll bring
To Him alone they'll always cling
His glories praise – forever sing!

Be thankful He loves Himself the most
He'll fill you with His Holy Ghost
And with His pleasures be engrossed
He's greatest joy from coast to coast
He's the delight of heaven's host
May He be your only boast!

Be thankful Christ is the center from Genesis to Revelation
He's the Word God spoke at the beginning of creation
And this Word became flesh in the glorious incarnation
He's the fourth man in the furnace of the Shadrach
conflagration
He's the greater Adam Who overcame the Devil's
temptation and passed the earthly probation
He's the greater Moses Who lead His people without
hesitation
Into the promised land where there'd be no tribulation
He's the greater David Who represented His congregation
In the great confrontation where He endured
condemnation to save them from damnation!

That's my King!

Be thankful for His Gospel every day
We need it for the power in all we do and say
It's not just for the beginning when we start to walk
Christ's way
But something to always live out in its manifold array
With our holy lives we must put it on display
It'll keep us from going astray
Help us pray, and we must always seek to give it away!

Be thankful for His lovely Bride
For her alone He bled and died
He always stands right by her side

CHRIST IS ALL!

She displays His beauty all worldwide
To principalities outside
Her every need He will provide
In glorious bliss she'll forever abide!

All the thanks you could ever render
Could never repay the Christ our Defender
He came and defeated every contender
He sends to endless hell every offender
And unmasks the heart of every pretender
So bow to Him by faith and surrender
And He'll fill your heart with everlasting splendor!

That's my King! I wonder if you know Him today?!

He's the God of the living Who conquered the grave
He puts an end to death's cold wave
Through the cross and resurrection He forgave
All sinners who repent and believe He'll save!

Mercy-Heart is His beautiful name
I'm so glad He took the shame and blame
That I should claim for my every wicked frame
But He became the same and by imputation my sin became
His Father's wrath He'd finally tame
So that "Freedom!" we could forever exclaim
If "Mercy!" too we'd cry and proclaim
May His glory alone be our only aim
All for the sake of the fame of His beautiful name!

He taught me "Christ is all!" through rejection and pain
And to boast only in the cross off the coast of Bahrain
So many earthly treasures I fought to attain
He taught me to live is Christ and to die is gain
May I wholly die now, fall to earth like a grain
Then fruit I'll produce that He can sustain
All praise and honor to the Lamb Who was slain
And with Him someday we'll forever reign
Then every reason for all the pain
In His love He'll forever make plain

CHRIST IS ALL!

As we enjoy His pleasures that will never wane!

That's my King! That's my King!

Every thing desirable and excellent in the union between
an earthly bridegroom and bride, is to be found in the
union between Christ and His church; and that in an
infinitely greater perfection and more glorious manner.
There is infinitely more to be found in it than ever was
found between the happiest couple in a conjugal relation;
or could be found if the bride and bridegroom had
not only the innocence of Adam and Eve,
but the perfection of angels.

Christ and His saints, standing in such a relation as this
one to another, the saints must needs be unspeakably
happy. Their mutual joy in each other is answerable to the
nearness of their relation and strictness of their union.
Christ rejoices over the church as the bridegroom rejoices
over the bride, and she rejoices in Him as the bride
rejoices over the bridegroom.

Jonathan Edwards

33
"THAT'S MY KING!"
WHO CUTS BUREAUCRACY
HUMBLES ARISTOCRACY
SHATTERS HYPOCRISY
AND RULES BY AUTOCRACY!

He despises man's ungodly tradition
To God's Word they seek to make an addition
But this is wholly contrary to Christ's mission
And will fuel His holy temper ignition
He has a relentless holy ambition
To save the self-righteous human condition
And bring godless sinners to His full submission
So don't put your hopes in any politician, physician,
superstition, or lofty recognition
But trust in Jesus' death and sin remission
By faith alone receive a righteous position
And acquire a growing holy disposition
That declares against all sin outright opposition
Because the beauty of Christ has no competition!

His disciples ate with defiled hands
But it's the heart the eye of the LORD scans
To see if in it righteousness stands

CHRIST IS ALL!

And holiness continues and expands
Just as the LORD promises and demands
God supplies grace to obey what He commands
And He'll make His sons many like the ocean sands!

That's my King!

Jesus came to set free – to cut down the complex
His burden is easy and shouldn't perplex
Jewish rules were more and less than God expects
Killing heart-worship was one of their effects
But if you see the glory Christ reflects
And the beauty His Person and work projects
You'll beg to be His royal subjects
Delighting in Him as the best of objects!

Worship that's vain is completely insane
It's like the unacceptable sacrifice of Cain
That's only profane
So break this evil chain
And turn to the Lamb Who was slain
But now lives with full reign
As the only One Who can end your pain
Worship Him from a pure heart to pleasure regain!

Hypocrisy He came to kill
True humility to instill
With unprecedented skill
He did His Father's perfect will
He died upon mount Calvary's hill
And rose up from the dead with zeal
The law and the prophets to fulfill
And open history's every seal
He Himself became our meal
And to His name all peoples kneel
Through His blood all nations heal
And He gives an everlasting thrill!

That's my King! I wonder if you know Him today?!

CHRIST IS ALL!

The Pharisees' hands had to be washed clean
Though their hearts were dirtier than a latrine
Outwardly they shine, clear, bright, and pristine
But inside they're dead and rotten gangrene
It's uglier than anything you've ever seen
Unless, of course, the Clean of cleans you've seen
Who makes even the dirtiest latrine clean, bright, and
pristine
Brings to life gangrene and clears it from the scene
For sinners He'd intervene
He's the mediator and the Father's go-between
In order to turn the ugliest into the most beautiful clean!

If your worship is fake
It's for your own sake
God's glory you take
Vile idols you make
You'll burn in the lake
Unless Christ makes you awake
Your sin forsake
Selfishness He'll break
And save you from heart ache
In His glory you'll partake
And your life He'll remake
Worship won't be fake
But done for His own name's sake!

God doesn't want honor merely from your lips
It's your whole life and heart He takes and grips
His delights flow down like the honeycomb drips
So come to Christ by faith and with joy He equips
From His river of pleasures you'll forever take sips
Where His glory will never suffer slips, trips, or eclipse!

That's my King!

God's holy commandments you shouldn't leave
But run to the glorious Christ and cleave
He saves if you'll only repent and believe
He died and rose, salvation to achieve

CHRIST IS ALL!

Dead, hell-bound sinners He came to retrieve
By His grace may you have new eyes to perceive
He lives for you now, your fears to relieve
He's the most precious gift you could ever receive
He's greater than all your mind could conceive!

He rules the world with almighty power
He's our refuge and strength, our strong High Tower
All of our enemies He'll finally devour
Though His tenderness and beauty bloom like a flower
May we be ready now, He returns any hour
Upon us great blessings He'll eternally shower!

That's my King! That's my King!

Oh Father, please help me claim no right to myself – no right to my understanding, my will, my affections; my body or its members – no right to my tongue, to my hands, my feet, my ears, my eyes, my sexuality and all my strong desires. They are all Yours and belong to You. You bought them with Your dear Son's blood. You own all of me oh God! Please use me as You please for Your own glory.

Please help me give myself clear away to You today and not retained anything of my own. I give myself wholly to You. May I give You every power, so that for the future I claim no right to myself in any respect. Only by Your grace I will not fail. Please help me take You alone as my whole portion and delight, looking upon nothing else as any part of my happiness. May Your law be the constant rule of my obedience.

Please help me fight with all my might against the world, the flesh, and the devil to the end of my life. Please help me adhere to the faith of the Gospel, however hazardous and difficult the profession and practice of it may be. Please grant me Your blessed Spirit as my Teacher, Sanctifier, and only Comforter, and cause me to cherish all admonitions to enlighten, purify, confirm, comfort, and assist me.

Please help me not to act in any respect as my own. Please keep me from using any of my powers to do anything that is not for Your glory. Please make Your glory the whole and entire business of my life. Please keep me from murmuring in the least at any afflictions; from being unkind in any way; from ever seeking revenge; from doing anything purely to please myself; from failing to do anything because it is a great self-denial; from trusting in myself; from accepting praise for any good which Christ does by me; and from being proud in any way. Please hear my prayer and answer for Jesus' sake! Amen!

Adapted Prayer from Jonathan Edwards

34
"THAT'S MY KING!"
WHO'S THE ONLY SAVING
PRESIDENT WHO CAN MAKE YOU
A HEAVENLY RESIDENT AND IN
PERFECT RIGHTEOUSNESS
REPRESENT!

My King was born President in the humble manger
For sin and righteousness He became the great Exchanger
To suffering, pain, and death He was no stranger
But He rose up from the dead to become the only true
world Changer
From sin, death, and hell He'll save you from all danger
And become your whole life's almighty Re-arranger!

He was elected by God as Head over His people
He died for His Church, and it's not a cathedral or wood
under a steeple
But a group of people who've miraculously walked through
the eye of a needle
And even though they're often feeble
By grace they wait on the LORD and mount up with wings
like an eagle!

CHRIST IS ALL!

Neither Obama nor Romney can save your soul
Only Jesus is worthy to open the scroll
Men make promises, but they all have a hole
Because there's just so much man can't control
But the omnipotent Christ rules over the whole
And He alone ought to be number one on your poll
You'll find in Him alone the One worthy to extol!

That's my King!

The poor and the rich, unborn babies and women, every
race and nation – He loves them all
He loves the politician who serves city hall
And the brick mason too who builds on the wall
He only demands that you heed His call
To repent and believe and before Him fall
Believe the Gospel, and He'll forever enthrall
As you take Him alone as your all in all!

He never spends more money than He has because He
owns everything
He's not left or right wing, but over the whole universe He's
sovereign King
The sun, moon, and stars from His hand He did fling
Trust in the Gospel now and to Him alone cling
He'll make your heart sing
From your lips His praises must ring
And to you fullness of joy and pleasures forevermore He'll
bring!

His budget is balanced all the time
He owns the whole world and every dime
He died to save sinners of any crime
And grant them a richness that's truly sublime
He's the executive, legislative, and judicial branch all at the
same time!

That's my King! Do you know Him?!

CHRIST IS ALL!

He executes every action that needs to be taken
He died on the cross your soul to awaken
Follow Him and you'll never be mistaken
His rule and government can never be shaken
If by faith you're His you'll never be forsaken!

He's the law itself Who's come down from above
He's God in the flesh Who's perfect love
He's gentle and tender, just like a dove!

He's also the righteous judge of all the earth
He'll condemn all people who are without new birth
So come and acknowledge His infinite worth
And He'll fill you with everlasting, unquenchable mirth!

He only speaks the truth and never lies
Just like He said He would die and then rise
And win for His people the everlasting prize
Now He never dies
In and of Himself He's infinitely wise
He'll never compromise or demise
And He has all the best allies
He never needs to improvise or revise
Because He has all-knowing, perfect eyes
Trust in Him, and He'll fill you with infinite supplies
He only satisfies and fills your life with delightful surprise!

That's my King!

He only does what's right
His record is out of sight
Against all your enemies He won the fight
He's your indestructible, shining Knight
Who's also the everlasting, unchanging Light
About Him you could infinitely write
He has all power and might
And can save from your hellish plight
So trust in Him on election night
And He'll usher in everlasting joy and delight!

CHRIST IS ALL!

Though Adam was our federal head
He sinned and left us all for dead
Bearing the burden – lifelong dread
Now only hell awaits ahead
But God has spoken, and this He said
"I won't leave my people dead
But elect a new federal Head
Who will obey and love instead!
He'll be the everlasting Bread
And stand in my peoples' stead
He'll take their place as the True Adam dead!"
And as to death a lamb is lead
Upon that cross He died and bled
But in Him all death finally fled
He rose from the grave and on death tread
And now salvation is widespread!

That's my King! That's my King!

What is the world to me
With all its vaunted pleasure
When Thou, and Thou alone,
Lord Jesus, art my Treasure!
Thou only, dearest Lord,
My soul's Delight shalt be;
Thou art my Peace, my Rest –
What is the world to me!

The world is like a cloud
And like a vapor fleeting,
A shadow that declines,
Swift to its end retreating.
My Jesus doth abide,
Though all things fade and flee;
My everlasting Rock –
What is the world to me!

The world abideth not;
Lo, like a flash 'twill vanish;
With all it gorgeous pomp
Pale death it cannot banish;
Its riches pass away,
And all its joys must flee;
But Jesus doth abide –
What is the world to me!

What is the world to me!
My Jesus is my Treasure,
My Life, my Health, my Wealth,
My Friend, my Love, my Pleasure,
My Joy, my Crown, my All,
My Bliss eternally.
Once more, then, I declare:
What is the world to me!

Georg M. Pfefferkorn

35
"THAT'S MY KING!"
WHO'S THE VETERAN OF VETERANS
WHO ANSWERED THE CALL AND
BECAME THE UNIVERSE'S
ALL IN ALL!

He's the only One Who perfectly served
God's law He always perfectly observed
And shed His blood for the undeserved!

He has infinite might
Won the greatest fight
Put all enemies to flight
Makes all wrongs right
And gives everlasting delight!

He's God's Ultimate Warrior Who never sins
He finishes everything He begins
His power and strength never thins
Against all enemies He defends
And always wins
With every threat He contends
And to hell He sends
So make amends

CHRIST IS ALL!

And by faith become one of His friends
To you His mercy extends
And then enjoy His beauty that forever transcends!

That's my King!

When I hit the buoy, He was there with me
Each event occurs according to His decree
Our ship was tossed about the Arabian Sea
But low and behold what did I see
A cross-shaped buoy – that bloody tree
May this memory from pride always set me free
May my boast be in Him to every degree
May all glory ever be to the great One in Three!

He's an army of One Who can't be beat
He's got more power than every navy fleet
He's better than all special forces elite
If you're on His side, you'll never face defeat
From the battle He'll never retreat
His supplies for the war never deplete
He'll never mistreat
With Him no one can compete
Every mission He'll perfectly complete
And save His people from everlasting heat!

That's my King! Do you know Him?!

For a few good men one may dare to die
But in this God shows His love so high
While we were still sinners, Christ died to buy
Salvation for all who would comply
So repent and believe – on Christ rely
He will be your everlasting supply!

He gave His life on the battle field
To all temptations He'd never yield
From the grave He rose and salvation sealed
And became our everlasting Shield
He lived and died and rose and healed

CHRIST IS ALL!

To the world His Father He perfectly revealed
He returns with a sword of judgment to wield
So trust in Him, and you won't be killed
But instead be forever thrilled
And with pleasures unspeakable be filled!

That's my King!

Every decoration He deserves and more
The Medal of Honor and all décor
He's more decorated than the whole Marine Corps
Alone on that cross He won the greatest war
To save our souls and earth restore
Now Him alone we'll forever adore
And find our delights eternally soar!

He won the battle against the great snake
Though His heal was bruised, the devil's head He'd break
The earth did quake
But He rose from the dead to end earth's ache
And finally cast the devil into the eternal, fiery lake
He'll make His dead people awake
And He did it all for His Father's great name's sake!

That's my King! That's my King!

243

Christ in the circle of His disciples would make them so happy that none would remark upon the [lack] of John or Peter. Christ as "Lamb in the midst of the throne" is able to give intense joy to millions upon millions, His look, voice, smile, presence. Oh to see "the King in His beauty!" We shall be sick of love, and yet find all health in that love.

"All my springs are in Thee."

It will be ecstasy to have made this attainment, to love the Lord our God with all our heart and soul and strength and mind . . . Those who have real love to Christ always wish they had more.

Of all things beware of a cold heart.

Christ will not let anything interfere with your love for Him.

He says, "I am all for you, and you must be all for Me."

Andrew Bonar

36
"THAT'S MY KING!"
WHO'S THE SON WHOSE BLOOD WAS
SPILLED SO BABIES WON'T BE
KILLED BUT INSTEAD LIVE
FULFILLED AND IN HIM
ALONE BE THRILLED!

There's a great evil in the world called abortion
In truth it's murder and that's not a distortion
Of all social evils it's out of proportion
Babies' blood for money – it's greedy extortion
Of parents' pure love it's a wicked contortion
Our only hope is finding Christ
as our all satisfying portion!

We want to rescue those who are to death taken away
Of all they're the most innocent and helpless – they have
no say
55 million dead and gone since the high court had its sway
Our great God said, "You shall not murder;" There's no
room for gray
But all of us in anger have murdered and gone astray
Our own sin on that cross the Son of God did slay

CHRIST IS ALL!

He's the most innocent and became helpless to obey
Innocence died on that cross and then rose to be the Way
He put God's love for murderers on manifold display
Now to us vast depths of mercy He forever does convey
And promises to never leave but always love and stay
To make known His breathless beauty to you in wide array
Which you will love and treasure and forevermore survey
So bow down to this great King –
cry, hope in Him, and pray
Make your grace filled choice –
repent and believe without delay
Turn from wicked idols and take Christ as your all today!

That's my King! Do you know Him?!

He gave Himself to satisfy the needs of the oppressed
Of all love givers He's the best
He bled and died to pass the test
Then rose up alive to fulfill His quest
If we believe in Him for rest
He'll save our souls and be our Guest
In His righteousness we will be dressed
And toward good works we will be pressed
We'll stand up for the weak distressed
And who could be more sore oppressed
Than babies doctors would molest
Instead of safe inside her nest
Or nursing at their mother's breast
They're dismembered upon request
Over this we should be depressed
Until our sins we do confess, detest, and leave dispossessed
Then in Christ we will be blessed
For all our sin has been addressed
We stood condemned with Christ our Rest
And rose with Him alive with zest
Now we live as those possessed
For with our Christ we are obsessed
For He's our living Treasure Chest!

CHRIST IS ALL!

So if you have an abortion past
There's grace for you that's unsurpassed
For where your sin has been amassed
His grace your sin will sure outlast
His love for you is great and vast
For on that cross it came to pass
God's own loved Son with wrath He'd blast
To save you from your wicked past
And your whole life He will recast
That's why this Christ is unsurpassed!

That's my King! That's my King!

If a man has Christ, then what does he [lack]? If a man has Christ, he has everything. If I [lack] perfection, and I have Christ, I have absolute perfection in Him. If I [lack] righteousness, I shall find in Him my beauty and my glorious dress. I [lack] pardon, and if I have Christ, I am pardoned. I [lack] heaven, and if I have Christ, I have the Prince of heaven, and shall be there by-and-by, to live with Christ, and to dwell in His blessed embrace forever. If you have Christ, you have all. Do not be desponding, do not give ear to the whisperings of Satan that you are not the children of God; for if you have Christ, you are His people, and other things will come by-and-by. Christ makes you complete in Himself; as the apostle says, "Ye are complete in Him."

Ye blind, ye lame, who are far from Christ, come to Him, and receive your sight, and obtain strength! He is made your all; you need bring nothing in your hand to come to Him.

Charles Spurgeon

37
"THAT'S MY KING!"
WHO ABOVE ALL IS THE GREATEST DREAM, WON CIVIL RIGHTS IN THE SUPREME, AND FROM ALL RACISM WILL REDEEM TO GRANT RACIAL HARMONY IN THE EXTREME!

Dream: Anything extremely beautiful, excellent, fine, or pleasant; Something that fully satisfies.[10]

Jesus alone is the Dream of dreams
He's glorious and beautiful in the extreme
In all excellence He's utterly supreme
He's more pleasant and sweet than the richest of cream
He's more pure and finer than any bright light gleam
He alone fully satisfies in His Kingdom regime
Of all redemption He's the great Theme
For He died and rose all peoples to redeem!

---

10 Ideas for this definition were taken from The American Heritage Dictionary of the English Language, Fifth Edition. http://www.thefreedictionary.com/Dream, Accessed 17 DEC 2015.

CHRIST IS ALL!

Martin Luther King had a dream he cried
His dream was good – we're on his side
Yet though he fought and bled and tried
In the end he was shot and died
We need a King Who'll still provide
One Who died then rose wide-eyed
To forevermore as King preside
O'er all the earth He reigns as guide
He won civil rights for His interracial Bride
And cast all racism aside
So we could praise His name worldwide
And now, in Him, if we abide
There's no more race or hate divide
He made us one – His race allied
He took us all from the outside
To make us family by His side
So set your racial pride aside
For "Christ is all!" because He died!

That's my King! I wonder if you know Him today?!

He won for us our greatest civil right
By faith we're heaven's citizens outright
Where all colors, tribes, and peoples delight
In Christ Who's joy's everlasting height
Against all death and hate He won the fight
As heaven's King and Holy-Warrior Knight
His love and grace are truly out of sight
Of this broken world He is the Light
He bore God's wrath and died to make it right
Then rose all your sadnesses to rewrite
And now to joy in Him He does invite
Regardless of your color if black or white
For all are one in Him as their chief delight!

Christ alone brings racial peace to every nation
His own marriage is a beautiful demonstration
The God-Man Jew wed to an all peoples combination
This – a glorious interracial celebration
The Church from every tribe and tongue and nation

CHRIST IS ALL!

Is the Bride He bought through death and resurrection
And one amazing realization of His propitiation for our
salvation
Is the total cessation of all racial segregation
For the glory of our King Who's the racial harmony
causation
Worthy of all praise and adoration
As our greatest preoccupation and fascination ruling over
every nation!

That's my King! That's my King!

The best preaching is, "We preach Christ crucified."

The best living is, "We are crucified with Christ."

The best man is a crucified man.

The more we live beholding our Lord's unutterable griefs, and understanding how He has fully put away our sin, the more holiness shall we produce.

The more we dwell where the cries of Calvary can be heard, where we can view heaven, and earth, and hell, all moved by His wondrous passion – the more noble will our lives become.

Nothing puts life into men like a dying Savior.

Get close to Christ, and carry the remembrance of Him about you from day to day, and you will do right royal deeds.

Come, let us slay sin, for Christ was slain.

Come, let us bury all our pride, for Christ was buried.

Come, let us rise to newness of life, for Christ has risen.

Let us be united with our crucified Lord in His one great object — let us live and die with Him, and then every action of our lives will be very beautiful.

Charles Spurgeon

38
"THAT'S MY KING!"
FOR WHOM WE COUNT ALL THINGS
AS LOSS NO MATTER THE COST AND
CONSIDER THEM DROSS BECAUSE
HE DIED ON THAT CROSS!

Oh how often in our flesh we trust
Hoping in self and our goodness we must
Pride in our background and race can't be hushed
To free us from this, Christ came to be crushed
And to turn us away from all worldly lust
When we stay near the cross our pride's brought to dust
And on Christ alone all our hopes are thrust
For He was made sin Who alone was just
True righteousness is ours in Christ robust
Our pride we then hate and renounce in disgust
May our passion for Christ in flames now combust!

That's my King!

This text was so hard for me to prepare
Because my heart with its truth just can't compare
Lose husband or wife or for what you most care
Lose a child or great dreams my heart it would tear

CHRIST IS ALL!

But nothing we lose of all earthly fare
Can come close to our Christ or even compare
When you lose everything and your life is bare
You're tempted to cry out "That's just not fair!"
But these feelings with the truth of God just don't square
To get what's fair would be hell in despair
But God is gracious – His mercy He'll share
If you trust in Christ that moment He'll spare
And promise you heaven to be with Him there
To do you good all your days with an oath He did swear
May more love to Christ be our constant prayer
So that "Christ is all!" we may truly declare!

That's my King! Do you know Him?!

For Jesus our precious Savior and King
We'll count all things dung and lose everything
As our greatest Treasure to Him alone cling
Because of the joy He'll forever bring
To make us delight and in ecstasy sing
His praises from our hearts forever shall ring
Of true satisfaction He's the life Spring!

All that we value that's close to our heart
For Christ we must willingly let it depart
He must be our First Love right from the start
His love and His beauty are clear off the chart
He's the only One with Whom we can't part
All your sad pains He'll transform like fine art!

That's my King!

Jesus Himself is of surpassing worth
Alone in Himself He's the Treasure of earth
Through Him all nations can have new birth
And live in harmony with unquenchable mirth!

CHRIST IS ALL!

Christ is greater than the racial pride chase
He died and rose to create one glorious race
Of all ethnic peoples one race by His grace
A people like family, but with a stronger embrace
For Christ's blood is thicker than biological base
In His Church He came all racial strife to erase
And fill us with love leaving no racism trace
When we count everything loss and delight in His face!

That's my King! That's my King!

And for this reason, because Christ is all in all. Christ is a Christian's all, his only Lord and Savior, and all his hope and happiness. And to those who are sanctified, one as well as another and whatever they are in other respects, He is all in all, the Alpha and Omega, the Beginning and the End: He is all in all things to them.

Matthew Henry

"Look to Me and be saved, all the ends of the earth" (Isa. 45:22). On this look to Christ, on this view of His glory, depends all our salvation. Therefore everything we need for our complete salvation is also communicated to us as we look to Him.

A constant view of the glory of Christ will revive our souls and cause our spiritual lives to flourish and thrive. Our souls will be revived by the transforming power with which beholding Christ is always accompanied. This is what transforms us daily into the likeness of Christ. So let us live in constant contemplation of the glory of Christ, and power will then flow from Him to us, healing all our [moral deterioration], renewing a right spirit in us and enabling us to abound in all the duties that God requires of us.

Faith will fix our souls in Christ Who will fill us with delight and satisfaction. This, in heaven, is perfect blessedness, for it is caused by the eternal vision of the glory of God in Christ. So the more we behold the glory of Christ by faith now, the more spiritual and the more heavenly will be the state of our souls.

The reason why the spiritual life in our souls decays and withers is because we fill our minds full of other things, and these things weaken the power of grace. But when the mind is filled with thoughts of Christ and His glory, these things will be expelled.

John Owen

39
"THAT'S MY KING!"
WHO HAS THE MOST INNOCENT BLOOD EVER SHED, TOOK GOD'S GREATEST WRATH UPON HIS HEAD, AND GRANTS MERCY TO ALL SINCE HE ROSE FROM THE DEAD!

Our God is filled with rage and hate
For those who make a child and mate
Then have her killed – a dreadful fate
Innocent blood was her pure state
For in the womb God does create
These precious little babes ornate
But toward God's image there is hate
Parents, their babe, will desecrate
Doctors kill while they sedate
And politicians' laws dictate
That murder is a choice – irate!
Against them all judgments await
But wrath doesn't have to be their fate
For all who turn and their sin hate
And trust in Christ as their soul mate
They shall be saved – there's no debate!

CHRIST IS ALL!

Our God is for us – He'll negate
All the lies accusers state
For Jesus died and bore the weight
Of all our sins that God does hate
He was crushed and took our fate
Then rose our lives to recreate
And now we're free – this should elate!
No condemnation does await!
For Christ our Savior is that great!

That's my King! Do you know Him?!

We must act for babies in the womb
55 million were sent to their doom
Against this evil we must fume
Submit to God and don't assume
Pray for new life to resume
Disciple and speak so death won't consume
Encourage adoption so there won't be gloom
Vote pro-life when you must choose whom
All for our King Who took our doom
Then rose alive up from the tomb
He loves the babies in the womb
He would be their loving Groom
Zeal for them does Him consume
End it all LORD – come back soon!

He's the only innocent in all the earth
His blood is of infinite, glorious worth
He shed His blood to give new birth!

That's my King!

Of all your loves, He's the greatest Treasure
His beauty and love are without measure
And He alone can give infinite pleasure!

CHRIST IS ALL!

So trust in Him – He'll remove all your sin
He will give new life within
No matter how many abortions have been
With Him a new life you'll begin
For He died and rose to win
And take away your every sin
He'll be your life and joy again!

That's my King! That's my King!

You recollect the old story we told, years ago, of Jack the converted huckster who used to sing: "I'm a poor sinner, and nothing at all, But Jesus Christ is my all in all."

Those who knew him were astonished at his constant composure. They had a world of doubts and fears, and so they asked him why he never doubted. "Well," he said, "I can't doubt but that I am a poor sinner, and nothing at all, for I know that, and feel it every day. And why should I doubt that Jesus Christ is my all in all? for He says He is." "Oh!" said his questioner, "I have my ups and downs." "I don't," said Jack; "I can never go up, for in myself I am a poor sinner, and nothing at all; and I cannot go down, for Jesus Christ is my all in all."

Jack wanted to join the church, and they said he must tell his conversion experience. He said, "All my experience is that I am a poor sinner, and nothing at all, and Jesus Christ is my all in all." "Well," they said, "when you come before the church meeting, the minister may ask you questions." "I can't help it," said Jack, "all I know I will tell you; and this is all I know: "I'm a poor sinner, and nothing at all, But Jesus Christ is my all in all."

He was admitted into the church, and continued with the brethren, walking in holiness; but that was still all his experience, and you could not get him beyond it. "Why," said one brother, "I sometimes feel so full of grace, I feel so advanced in sanctification, that I begin to be very happy." "I never do," said Jack; "I am a poor sinner, and nothing at all." "But then," said the other, "I go down again, and think I am not saved, because I am not as sanctified as I used to be." "But I never doubt my salvation," said Jack, "because Jesus Christ is my all in all, and He never alters." That simple story is grandly instructive, for it sets forth a plain man's faith in a plain salvation; it is the likeness of a soul under the apple tree, resting in the shade, and feasting on the fruit.

Charles Spurgeon

40
"THAT'S MY KING!"
WHO'S WORTHY OF ALL ADORATION, RANSOMED PEOPLE FROM EVERY NATION, AND WILL ACCOMPLISH PERFECT RACIAL RECONCILIATION!

Jesus Christ is the interracial King
His bride is a little bit of everything
And from His heart all love will spring
He died all peoples together to bring
Asian, African, and those in Beijing
By faith all as one to Him we'll cling
Join your voices and to Him sing!
"Worthy is the Lamb!" shall loudly ring!
There's no One like Him – our glorious King!
Who will forever make us sing!

Some believe racism is totally dead
It's no longer a problem some have said
If you believe that, you've been misled
For in our hearts this evil's spread
Denial won't help the past we've led
But on our enemies Christ will tread!
To cleanse our hearts His blood He shed!

CHRIST IS ALL!

A Lamb to the slaughter He was led
Beaten, bruised with wrath He bled
And then was raised up from the dead
Our racist thoughts He will behead
And we will love each race instead
And be a family – He's the Head
If we'll confess this sin we've fed
And trust the Son Who for us bled
To the King of race we'll wed
He'll be our Husband Who will shred
Each racist thought we've ever bred
He'll set us free to love widespread
From every tribe and tongue who's fled
Into His arms just as He said
And then there's only peace ahead
For He died to kill the dread
And leave racism fully dead!

That's my King! I wonder if you know Him today?!

Jesus is worthy to open the scroll
For He was slain to save your soul
He alone has met God's goal
He's God the man Who takes control
He has no sin – He's perfect – whole
He's the only righteous soul
If you trust Him, He'll console
He alone can make you whole
And He alone can save your soul
So turn to Him – give Him control
In all of life, Him you'll extol!

He ransomed people from every nation
We have them here – Chinese and Haitian
And the only hope for reconciliation
Is for Christ the Lamb to be our Fixation
As we look to His throne in holy fascination
He must be our race Foundation
His blood is thicker than any relation
So look to Him – the Author of creation

CHRIST IS ALL!

He'll make us one without condemnation
He'll move us to love without hesitation
There will be no more types of segregation
Martin Luther King's dream will find consummation
As we look to the Lamb with exclamation
And cry "You are worthy!" in pure admiration
Peace evermore will be our habitation
As we reign with our King with no more temptation
But only more joy and love escalation
While we worship the Lamb with every nation!

That's my King! That's my King!

What, then, is the faith? Strange to say, the faith of Christians is a Person. You may ask all other religions wherein their faith lieth, and they cannot answer on this wise. Our faith is a Person; the Gospel that we have to preach is a Person, and go wherever we may, we have something solid and tangible to preach. If you had asked the twelve apostles, in their day, "What do you believe in?" they would not have needed to go round about with a long reply, but they would have pointed to their Master, and they would have said, "We believe Him."

"But what are your doctrines?"
"There they stand incarnate."

"But what is your practice?
"There stands our practice. He is our example."

"What, then, do you believe?"
Hear ye the glorious answer of the apostle Paul:
"We preach Christ crucified."

Our creed, our body of divinity, our whole theology is summed up in the person of Christ Jesus.

The apostle preached doctrine, but the doctrine was Christ. He preached practice, but the practice was all in Christ.

There is no summary of the faith of a Christian that can compass all he believes, except that word Christ – and that is the Alpha and the Omega of our creed, that is the first and the last rule of our practice – Christ, and Him crucified.

To spread the faith, then, is to spread the knowledge of Christ crucified. It is, in fact, to bring men, through the agency of God's Spirit, to feel their need of Christ, to seek Christ, to believe in Christ, to love Christ, and then to live for Christ.

Charles Spurgeon

41
"THAT'S MY KING!"
WHOSE BLOOD WAS OUT POURED
AS THE COVENANT LORD
SO WE'RE CLEAN AND RESTORED
THROUGH OUR CHRIST THE
REWARD WHO'S ALWAYS AND ONLY
AND EVER ADORED!

In a heated rage man's blood was shed
Cain killed his brother Abel dead
In envy-lust the ground soaked red
It cried to God, "you're cursed," God said
Sin causes death, from God we've fled
But there's a promise we have read
The Seed will crush the serpent's head
He suffered on that cross and bled
Then conquered death and left it dead!

The life is in the blood, so you shall not eat
The blood of bulls and goats that bleat
Jews could only eat the meat
Or be cut off – their hopes delete
But blood of bulls and goats won't treat

CHRIST IS ALL!

The sickness – sin has brought defeat
We need a greater hope complete
It's in the blood of Christ elite
His life and death – the greatest feat
On that cross we did mistreat
The LORD of glory Who they beat
His blood poured out like slaughtered meat
He bore God's wrath in all its heat
Then rose to conquer all defeat
And cause the devil to retreat
Now by His blood we are complete
He gave Himself – His blood so sweet!
We shout with joy in the street!
His praise always we'll now repeat!

That's my King! Do you know Him?!

Jesus' blood of the New Covenant is our propitiation
He took away God's wrath, so that we could have salvation
Because He died and rose for our eternal justification
He's the New Covenant LORD Who's our bloody mediation
So now we're forgiven and enjoy God's "Righteous!"
declaration
Which we have by faith alone in the Christ our blood
relation
Now there's no more fear of wrath – no hell-fire or
damnation
Through His blood we have redemption from all sinful
desolation
From every nation we're brought near by His blood of
consecration
Through His blood we now have peace so there's no more
agitation
The precious blood of Christ Who is our Lamb of jubilation
Cleanses us from sin so there's no more indignation
By His blood we're freed from sin to live out holy
dedication

CHRIST IS ALL!

By His blood alone there will be no more condemnation
And by His blood alone we'll conquer every manifestation
and representation of our enemies' perpetration
For the glory of our King Who's our joy and adoration!

That's my King! That's my King!

The love of Jesus answered by our love to Jesus makes
the sweetest music the heart can know. No joy on earth is
equal to the bliss of being all taken up with love to Christ.
If I had my choice of all the lives that I could live, I
certainly would not choose to be an emperor, nor to be a
millionaire, nor to be a philosopher; for power, and wealth,
and knowledge bring with them sorrow and travail; but I
would choose to have nothing to do but to love my Lord
Jesus – nothing, I mean, but to do all things for His sake,
and out of love to Him. Then I know that I should be in
paradise, yea, in the midst of the paradise of God, and I
should have meat to eat which is all unknown to men of the
world. Heaven on earth is abounding love to Jesus.
This is the first and last of true delight — to love
Him Who is the First and the Last. To love
Jesus is another name for paradise.

Charles Spurgeon

42
S. M. LOCKRIDGE AND
IT'S FRIDAY, BUT
SUNDAY'S COMIN'!

Another powerful, prophetic, passionate, poetic plea from
Dr. S. M. Lockridge is called "It's Friday, But Sunday's
comin'!" I have imitated his style in this plea at the end of
many of my sermons to drive the main point home. This
chapter contains this wonderful plea by Dr. Lockridge, and
then several chapters follow that I have written following
his powerful, poetic pattern.

It's Friday
Jesus is praying
Peter's a sleeping
Judas is betraying
But Sunday's comin'!

It's Friday
Pilate's struggling
The council is conspiring
The crowd is vilifying
They don't even know
That Sunday's comin'!

CHRIST IS ALL!

It's Friday
The disciples are running
Like sheep without a shepherd
Mary's crying
Peter is denying
But they don't know
That Sunday's a comin'!

It's Friday
The Romans beat my Jesus
They robe Him in scarlet
They crown Him with thorns
But they don't know
That Sunday's comin'!

It's Friday
See Jesus walking to Calvary
His blood dripping
His body stumbling
And His spirit's burdened
But you see, it's only Friday
Sunday's comin'!

It's Friday
The world's winning
People are sinning
And evil's grinning

It's Friday
The soldiers nail my Savior's hands
To the cross
They nail my Savior's feet
To the cross
And then they raise Him up
Next to criminals

It's Friday
But let me tell you something
Sunday's comin'!

CHRIST IS ALL!

It's Friday
The disciples are questioning
What has happened to their King
And the Pharisees are celebrating
That their scheming
Has been achieved
But they don't know
It's only Friday
Sunday's comin'!

It's Friday
He's hanging on the cross
Feeling forsaken by His Father
Left alone and dying
Can nobody save Him?

Ooooh
It's Friday
But Sunday's comin'!

It's Friday
The earth trembles
The sky grows dark
My King yields His spirit

It's Friday
Hope is lost
Death has won
Sin has conquered
and Satan's just a laughin'

It's Friday
Jesus is buried
A soldier stands guard
And a rock is rolled into place

But it's Friday
It is only Friday
Sunday is a comin'!

I am persuaded there are more delights in Christ, yes, more joy in one glimpse of His face, than is to be found in all the praises of this harlot-world and in all the delights that it can yield in its sunniest and brightest days . . .

Are you poor, my dear brother? Do you see Jesus? He was poorer than you. You have somewhere to sleep tonight, but He could say, "Foxes have holes, and birds of the air have nests, but the Son of Man has nowhere to lay His head?" (Luke 9:58). Are you racked with pain? Let it help you to see Jesus. You are not "exceedingly sorrowful, even to death" (Matt. 26:38), nor is your grief to be compared with His. Have you been betrayed and deserted? See Jesus as He is kissed by Judas (Matt. 26:49). Have you been denied by some friend who promised to be faithful? Look into the face of Jesus as He turns to Peter (Luke 22:61). Is death staring you in the face? Remember Him Who "being found in appearance as a man, humbled Himself and became obedient to the point of death, even the death of the cross" (Phil. 2:8). We would never be alone if we could see Jesus; or if we were alone it would be a blessed solitude. We would never feel deserted if we could see Jesus; or if we were deserted we would have the best of helpers. If we could always see Jesus we would not feel weak for He would be our strength and our song. Oh to see Jesus! You have seen Him as Your Savior, and you desire to see Him as Your Master. Oh to see Him as a friend on whom you can still lean your aching head, someone into whose ear you can pour your [story] of sorrow! Through this wilderness, you may continually lean on Him and have perpetual sweet enjoyment. Then this earth, desert as it is, will seem to blossom like a garden of roses, and your spirit will enjoy heaven below.

Charles Spurgeon

43
IT'S SUNDAY, BUT
HIS RETURN IS COMIN'!

It's Sunday
The devil couldn't defeat Him
Sin couldn't stop Him
Death couldn't handle Him
And the grave couldn't hold Him!
And His return is comin'!

It's Sunday
The tomb is empty
The grave clothes are folded
The stone has been removed
The Son has risen
His work is finished
And we all know
That His return is comin'!

It's Sunday
Hope has been restored
Sin has been conquered
Death has been defeated
The strong man has been bound

CHRIST IS ALL!

Now all the nations will come to Him
Before His return is comin'!

It's Sunday
Mary is crying
The disciples are trembling
But soon they'll be rejoicing
Then they'll be a preaching
And tellin' the whole world about Him
Callin' all men everywhere to repent and believe in Him
Because His return is comin'!

It's Sunday
The priests are bribing
The elders are lying about what happened
The soldiers are telling stories
And the Jews are believing the lie that His body was stolen
But His return is comin'!

It's Sunday
On the Emmaus road
Jesus new light has bestowed
From Moses to the prophets He has showed
It's all about Him – the Word is sowed
All allegiance to Him is fully owed
Because His return is comin'!

It's Sunday
Thomas is doubting
But soon he'll be a shouting
As he touches the scars of his dear Savior
And then He'll be declaring
Jesus as his Lord and his God
And someday all will be proclaiming
Either willingly or unwillingly
That Jesus Christ is Lord!
Because His return is comin'!

CHRIST IS ALL!

It's Sunday
Peter has gone fishing
Ashamed that he denied his Master
But soon he'll be restored
Oh Peter, do you love Me?
Yes, soon he'll be restored
By His loving, merciful, and patient King
Who will send Him to feed His sheep
Because His return is comin'!

It's Sunday
His disciples will be commissioned
To teach others to obey all He has commanded
And all but one of them will die
To lift His name on high
But all their enemies don't know
That His return is comin'!

It's Sunday, but His return is comin'
Are you ready?
He's coming back on a white war horse to make war
His name is Faithful and True and The Word of God
His eyes are like a flame of fire
A sharp sword comes out of His mouth
He will tread the winepress of the fury of the wrath of God
the Almighty
People will cry out for mountains and rocks to fall on them
to shield them from the wrath of the Lamb
His wrath and judgment are coming
It's only Sunday, there's time for you to turn from your
sins, trust in Him, and accept His terms of peace
It's only Sunday, but His return is comin'!

It's Sunday
The new creation has begun
There is now no condemnation for those at peace in Him
All our sins have been forgiven
God has cast them behind His back
And He remembers them no more

CHRIST IS ALL!

As far as the east is from the west, He has removed our sins
from us
He has cast them onto the ocean floor
We are now to walk in the newness of holy lives
We are no longer slaves to sin, but slaves to righteousness
Because His return is comin'!

It's Sunday
All things are now working for our good
Nothing can separate us from the love of God in Christ
Jesus
In Christ all things are ours
And though there's still a lot of pain and suffering
His return is comin'!

It's Sunday
Sin is still tempting
The world is still deceiving
The flesh is still warring
The devil is still prowling
Children are still being abused and dying
Racism is still dividing
Cancer is still killing
Wombs are still barren
Marriage is still hard
Singleness is still lonely
Hopes are still deferred
Dreams are still broken
But His return is comin'!

It's Sunday
People are still poor
Loved ones still die
Tragedies still undo us
Crime is still rampant
Abortion is still killing
Airplanes are still disappearing
Ferry boats are still sinking
All manner of heart-breaks are still happening
Tears are still flowing

CHRIST IS ALL!

But let me tell you something
His return is comin'!

And on that great day! Oooh on that great day of the
everlasting wedding day
He will wipe away every tear from your eyes
There will be no more sin
There will be no more death
There will be no more pain
There will be no more heart-break of any kind
There will be no more loss or loneliness
There will be no more sadness but only ever increasing joy
for all eternity
There will be a new heavens and a new earth where only
perfect, perpetual, pure righteousness dwells
The earth will be filled with the knowledge of the glory of
the LORD as the waters cover the sea
You will be eternally saved, safe, and satisfied[11] beyond
your greatest imagination
And everything sad will become untrue![12]

It's Sunday
It's only Sunday
But His return is a comin'!

---

11 John Piper used this phrase in the funeral sermon he gave for
    his father on March 9, 2007.
    http://www.desiringgod.org/conference-messages/funeral-
    message-for-william-s-h-piper Accessed 21 JAN 2015.

12 This phrase comes from J.R.R. Tolkien in *The Return of the
    King*.

I once thought I was a Christian, in the truth I believed
Then through a teacher I found I was deceived
He was teaching us world religions
But to him they're all relative you see
"All religions are roads to the same god for me"
This teaching was against all I learned
From mom and Sunday school
I learned that salvation through
Jesus Christ alone was the rule
Fear entered my heart, I was more than afraid
I began to doubt that Jesus alone was my aid
If I couldn't believe in Jesus alone as Savior and Lord
"I'll go to hell forever!" my mind unceasingly roared
I just believed because my mom taught me so
Would an Indian child believe what I know?
I struggled and struggled to find
The belief I thought I had but then lost
But in truth, the river from death to life
Through saving faith I had never crossed
Now I understand Jesus' words Luke did pen
Agonizing and striving are required
For the straight gate to enter in
After much pain and fear of death and eternal suffering
By God's grace I embraced Jesus as second to nothing
Looking back one thing seems very, very clear
Relativism is a deadly, false teaching to fear
African, Asian, Indian, or Arab no cultures are exempt
All peoples are commanded to turn
To Jesus alone and repent
The hope of this truth resides not in man's effort or will
But in an Almighty God Who gives new hearts with a seal
Now in Jesus alone I find my delights soar and soar
Very soon with Him I'll find pleasures forevermore!
Now if you have ears to hear and eyes to see
Your future so grim
Run to Jesus right now
And find fullness of joy in Him!

Joseph Randall

44
IT'S CHRISTMAS, BUT
THE CROSS IS COMIN'!

It's Christmas
A virgin is pregnant
Joseph is wondering what happened
The Angel Gabriel is making the story clear
But the cross is comin'!

It's Christmas
Women who can't get pregnant are rejoicing
The impossible is becoming possible
God is acting
The Holy Spirit is overshadowing
Songs of praise are being written
But the cross is comin'!

CHRIST IS ALL!

It's Christmas
The Mighty One has done great things
His mercy is from generation to generation
He's scattering the proud
He's toppling the mighty
He's satisfying the hungry
And sending the rich away empty
Because they don't know
That the cross is comin'!

It's Christmas
The God of Israel has visited to provide redemption for His
people
He has raised up a horn of salvation to save us from our
enemies and all who hate us
He'll bring us knowledge of salvation and forgiveness of
our sins
Light is going to shine in darkness
Because the cross is comin'!

It's Christmas
Caesar Augustus is decreeing
Joseph and Mary are traveling
The cattle are feeding
Herod is conniving
The Star is shining
Angels are speaking
The shepherds are praising
But the cross is comin'!

It's Christmas
No room was found in the inn for my King
No bed was available where He could lay His head
He's homeless
He's laying in the feeding trough of a cow
But they don't even know
That the cross is comin'!

CHRIST IS ALL!

It's Christmas
The glory of the Lord is shining
Good news of great joy for all people is being proclaimed
A Savior Who is Christ the Lord is born
Glory to God in the highest and peace on earth
Because the cross is comin'!

It's Christmas
The shepherds are preaching about the glory of my King
All who hear them are amazed
Mary is treasuring and meditating
But she doesn't know yet
That the cross is comin'!

It's Christmas
Wise men are seeking Him
The star He created –
The star He upholds by the Word of His power –
The star that can't compare with the brightness of His glory
That star is leading them to Him – the Savior of the world
And they shower Him with gifts: gold, frankincense, and
myrrh
But let me tell you something
The cross is comin'!

It's Christmas
Wickedness is abounding
Sin has no remedy
Herod is killing all the little babies
Mothers are weeping
Fathers are stumbling
There's no peace on earth
No justice is being done
But you see, it's only Christmas
The cross is comin'!

CHRIST IS ALL!

It's Christmas
Hope is born
Salvation has come
Prophecy has been fulfilled
God has become man
Yet He's the Sign Who will be opposed
And a sword will pierce Mary's heart
Because the cross is comin'!

It's Christmas
Joy to the world, the Lord has come
Sing choirs of angels, sing in exultation
Glory to the new born King
He rules the world with truth and grace
See within a manger laid, Jesus, Lord of heaven and earth
Oh come let us adore Him
Let every heart prepare Him room
And go tell it on the mountain
Because the cross is comin'!

It's Christmas
It's only Christmas
But the cross is comin'!

He is greater than any ruler . . .
mightier than any warrior . . .
nobler than any king . . .
wiser than any sage . . .
bigger than any kingdom . . .
better than any crown . . .
lovelier than any name . . .
worthy of worship . . .
deserving of praise.

Roy Lessin

The enjoyment of God is the only happiness with which our
souls can be satisfied. To go to heaven, fully to enjoy God,
is infinitely better than the most pleasant accommodations
here. Fathers and mothers, husbands, wives, or children,
or the company of earthly friends, are but shadows; but
God is the substance. These are but scattered beams, but
God is the sun. These are but streams.
But God is the ocean.

Jonathan Edwards

45
"THAT'S MY KING!"
WHO'S THE PASSOVER LAMB
THE SUBSTITUTE RAM,
AND THE GREAT "I AM"
SO WE CAN BE CHILDREN
OF ABRAHAM!

We've been passed over
The Lamb has been slaughtered
Blood has been poured out
Sin has been atoned for
The wrath of God has been quenched
Because Jesus was not passed over!

We've been passed over
Judgment upon sin has been executed
The curse of God has fallen
Hell's flames toward us have been extinguished
The Lamb of God has taken away the sin of the world
Because Jesus was not passed over!

CHRIST IS ALL!

We've been passed over
Just like God's people in Egypt were passed over
The lamb without blemish was slain
The blood of lambs was put on the doorposts
Those in the house were saved, safe, and satisfied[13]
While the first born child in every Egyptian house was
destroyed
All the first born children of Israel were kept alive
The LORD and His destroyer passed over their homes
But Jesus was not passed over!

We've been passed over
Even though we don't deserve to be passed over
Like undeserving Israel, we complain and murmur against
God
We don't love Him as we ought
We don't trust Him as we ought
We don't delight in Him as we ought
We don't obey Him as we ought
We don't love our neighbors as ourselves as we ought
And we sin as we ought not
But oh don't you know – by the finished work of the
Lord Jesus Christ it's all been taken care of forever
Because Jesus was not passed over!

We've been passed over
God's curse has passed over us
God's wrath has passed over us
God's judgment has passed over us
God's hell has passed over us
God's eternal and infinite condemnation has passed over
us forever
Because Jesus was not passed over!

---

13 John Piper used this phrase in the funeral sermon he gave for
    his father on March 9, 2007.
    http://www.desiringgod.org/conference-messages/funeral-
    message-for-william-s-h-piper Accessed 21 JAN 2015.

CHRIST IS ALL!

We've been passed over
But Jesus was wickedly turned over
Judas betrayed Him over
Pilate unjustly condemned Him over
Peter denied Him over and over and over
The soldiers mocked, beat, and spit on Him all over
Our sins were counted as His all over
Even His Father forsook Him as He cried out to Him over
and over
And wicked men and the devil thought it was all over
Because Jesus was not passed over!

But let me tell you something – it is not over!

We've been passed over
But let me tell you that when Jesus died on that cross it
was not all over
Oh tell yourself this over and over – that it's not over – it's
never over because of Jesus our Passover!

Whatever good you think is over in your life – dead and
hopeless and lifeless and over – it's not over because of
Jesus our Passover!
Because He came to turn over what's over and make all
things new over; He gives you a do-over; And can do the
ultimate make-over that will leave you praising Him over
and over!

For He has been raised up over all that seems over and
rules over all with all authority over heaven and over earth!
Because Jesus was not passed over!

We've been passed over
Because Jesus rose up from the dead and rules as King
over death!
He rules as King over sin!
He rules as King over the grave!
He rules as King over Satan!
He rules as King over the world!
He rules as King over our flesh!

CHRIST IS ALL!

He rules as King over all His and your enemies!
He rules as King over all as the Christ Who is all in all!
All because He was not passed over!

We've been passed over
So now we live to tell about Christ our Passover Who was
not passed over!
The same Holy Spirit that raised Him from the dead to rule
and reign over all is dwelling in you!
He grants you power over death!
He grants you power over sin!
He grants you power over the grave!
He grants you power over Satan!
He grants you power over the world and the flesh!
He grants you power over all of your enemies, so that you
are more than conquerors through Him Who loves you!

Oh you've been passed over because our God so loved you
that He gave His only begotten Son, so that whosoever
believes in Him shall not perish but have everlasting life!

Oh, yes – we've been passed over!
Because Jesus, our Passover, was not passed over!

Surely if He would not spare His own Son one stroke, one tear, one groan, one sigh, one circumstance of misery, it can never be imagined that ever He should, after this, deny or withhold from His people, for whose sakes all this was suffered, any mercies, any comforts, any privilege, spiritual or temporal, which is good for them.

John Flavel

You see, Madam, how precarious and uncertain all things here are! Live beside the creatures while you have them — let Christ be the all of your enjoyment in them — and then, when they fail, and your own heart and flesh too, Christ will be your all in Himself — the strength of your heart, and your portion forever — an all of bliss and glory, ineffable and eternal. Value your own Lord Jesus. Let His price (His worth in your esteem) be far above rubies, and all creatures and things, desirable and desired. The all-beauteous Godhead is in Him. He is the mighty God, as well as the Man Jesus, for you. Emanuel is His wonderful, glorious name. His personal and relative glories are, and shall be, the wonder and praise of men and angels unto ages without end. Look upon His lovely face — there is not another such beauty in both worlds! See, Madam, this is your Beloved, and this is your Friend. This is He Who has loved you, and given Himself for you; that laid aside His glory and joy, who was the adoration of angels, and the darling of the Father's bosom, to clothe Himself, His matchless Self, with your sin, shame, and sorrow, that He might raise you from the ash-heap of sinful nature to inherit with Him the joys and glories of the upper world; yes, to set you with Him upon His own throne! Oh, dear Madam, you are the Lamb's bride, even you, who come unto God, as the God of peace, only by and through the sacrificed Lamb. Admire the Lamb's love — the Lamb who was slain for you, that has wooed and won and betrothed you to Himself forever. Live upon Him, live to Him, and long to live with Him.

Anne Dutton

46
THE INCOMPARABLE KING
BY SAMUEL JONES

Another very powerful description of the incomparable Christ has been passed down to us by Samuel Jones, an evangelist at the close of the 19th century in America. This chapter contains his breathtaking description. He writes:

More than 2000 years ago there was a man born contrary to the laws of nature. He laid aside His purple robe for a peasant's tunic. He was rich, yet for our sake He became poor. This man lived in poverty and was raised in obscurity. He received no formal education and never possessed wealth or widespread influence. He never traveled extensively. He seldom crossed the boundary of the country in which He lived and that was during exile in His childhood. His relatives were inconspicuous, not influential, and had neither training nor education.

In infancy, He startled a king; in childhood, He amazed religious scholars; in manhood, He ruled over the course of nature, walked on stormy waves as if pavement, and hushed the raging sea to sleep. He healed the multitudes without medicine and made no charge for His services.

CHRIST IS ALL!

He never wrote a book, and yet all the libraries of the world hold books written about Him. He never wrote a song, and yet He has furnished the theme for more songs than all the songwriters combined. He never founded a college, but all the schools put together do not have as many students as does He. He never practiced medicine, and yet He has healed more broken hearts than all the doctors throughout history. He never marshaled an army, nor drafted a soldier, nor fired a gun, and yet no leader ever had more volunteers who have, under His orders, fought against truth's enemies.

He is the Star of astronomy

The Rock of geology

The Lion and the Lamb of the zoological kingdom

He is the Revealer of snares that lurk in the darkness

The Rebuker of every evil thing that prowls by night

The Promoter of all that is wholesome

The Adorner of all that is beautiful

The Reconciler of all that is contradictory

The Harmonizer of all discords

The Healer of all diseases, and the only Savior of all mankind.

He fills the pages of theology, hymnology, and the book of Psalms. Every prayer that goes up to God goes in His name and is asked to be granted for His sake.

The names of the proud statesmen of Egypt and Babylon and Greece and Rome and every other earthly kingdom have come and gone. The names of the past scientists, philosophers, and theologians have come and gone; but the name of this Man is still relevant and powerful and shall forever be so!

Though time has spread 2000 years between the people of this generation and the scene of His death, yet He still lives. Herod could not kill Him! Satan could not seduce Him! Death could not hold Him!

He stands forth upon the highest pinnacle of heavenly glory, proclaiming God, acknowledged by the angels, adored by saints, and feared by the demons, as a living, personal Christ.

A study of the Bible reveals Christ as its central Subject and great Theme. What the hub is to the wheel, Christ is to the Bible. It revolves around Him. All its stories point to Him; all its truths converge in Him; all its glories reflect Him; all its promises radiate from Him; all its beauties are embodied by Him; all its demands are exemplified by Him; and all its predictions are realized through Him.

Abel's lamb, that first sacrifice to God, was a type of Christ.

Abraham's offering of Isaac on Mount Moriah was a foretaste of God giving Christ on Mount Calvary. The Passover Lamb in Egypt was a type of Christ.

The bronze serpent in the wilderness that Moses held up for the people's healing was a type of Christ.

The scapegoat of Old Testament times symbolized Him bearing the sins of the world.

He was with Adam and Eve in the Garden of Eden. He was with Abel at his death. He walked with Enoch. He floated with Noah in the ark. He ate with Abraham in his desert tent. He fled with Lot to escape wicked Sodom.

He watched Isaac reopen the wells that his father Abraham

had dug. He wrestled with Jacob at Peniel. He strengthened Joseph in the time of temptation, protected him in prison, and exalted him to first place in the kingdom of Egypt. He watched over Moses as he floated in a basket among the bulrushes, talked to him from the burning bush, led him back to Egypt, opened the Red Sea for him, fed him with heaven's bread, protected him with a column of fire and finally led him to the top of Mount Nebo for a vision of the Promised Land and his eternal rest.

He was at Joshua's side as he crossed the Jordan and the Promised Land became a reality. He was with Gideon and his 300 men. He was with Samuel as he crowned Saul and David as kings of Israel. He was with David as he faced the giant. He was with Solomon building the first Temple. He was with King Hezekiah as Sennacherib, the Assyrian, invaded the land. He was with King Josiah as he restored the worship of Yahweh. He was with Ezekiel and Daniel in Babylon. He was with Ezra and Nehemiah as they returned from Babylon to rebuild Jerusalem and its wall. He was with all those who, through faith, subdued kingdoms, brought righteousness, stopped the mouths of lions, and out of their weakness were made strong by the mighty hand of God.

Abraham heard His voice while living in the desert of Ur of Chaldea. Jacob called Him the "Lawgiver of Judah." Moses called him "The Prophet that was to come." Job called Him, "My living Redeemer." Daniel called Him the "Ancient of Days." Isaiah called Him, "Wonderful Counselor, the Mighty God, the Everlasting Father, and the Prince of Peace."

Is all of this in the Old Testament? Yes, and much more besides. Micah tells of the place of His birth. Jonah tells of His death, burial, and resurrection. Amos tells of His second coming to build again the tabernacles of David. Joel describes the day of His wrath. Zechariah tells of His coming reign as King over all the earth. Every page is filled with Him! Its sacrifices show Him, its symbols signify

Him, its histories are His stories, its songs are His sentiments, its prophesies are His pictures, its promises are His pledges, and our hearts burn within us as we walk beside Him across its living pages!

Concerning His royal lineage, He was born in Bethlehem, the Seed of Abraham, the Son of David, the Son of Mary, and the Son of God. He was acknowledged as "King of the Jews," "Christ the Lord," "God's Son," "The Savior of Men," by angels, shepherds, demons, and wise men.

Concerning His service, we learn that He labored as a carpenter, opened the eyes of the blind, unstopped the ears of the deaf, loosed the mute tongues, cleansed lepers, restored withered hands, fed the hungry, sympathized with the sad, washed the disciple's feet, wept with Mary and Martha, preached the gospel to the poor, and gave His life on that cross.

He was born of a woman, as a little babe, He was wrapped in swaddling clothes, grew up and developed in wisdom and stature and in favor with God and man. He worked with His hands. He grew weary. He got hungry. He got thirsty. He slept. He got angry. He shed tears. He sweat great drops of blood. He was betrayed, went through the mockery of a trial, was whipped, His hands and His feet were pierced; He wore a crown of thorns, was spit upon, was crucified, was buried in a borrowed tomb behind a sealed stone, and was guarded by Roman soldiers.

He was born of a virgin, lived a sinless life, spoke matchless words, stilled storms, calmed waves, rebuked winds, multiplied loaves, turned water into wine, raised the dead, foretold the future, healed diseases, forgave sin, claimed equality with God, arose from the dead, and possesses all authority in heaven and on earth.

He is both God and man. As the God-man, He was thirsty, and yet He gave living water. He went to a wedding and turned the water into wine. He slept in a boat, yet He stilled the storm. He was tempted, yet He sinned not. He wept, yet He raised Lazarus from the dead. He prayed to the Father, and He also makes intercession for all His people.

This is what Paul means when he writes, "Great is the mystery of godliness; God was manifested in the flesh, justified by the Spirit, seen of angels, preached unto the Gentiles, believed on in the world, received up into glory" (1 Timothy 3:16). He is the Bread of Life and The Light of the World. He is the True Vine and the Good Shepherd. He is the Way, the Truth, and the Life! He is the Door to Heaven!

He is the Faithful Witness, the King of Kings, the Lord of Lords, Alpha and Omega, the Lord Who was and is and is to come! He is the Savior of the world!

In Genesis, He is the Seed of the woman.

In Exodus, He is the Passover Lamb.

In Leviticus, He is our High Priest.

In Numbers, He is the Pillar of cloud by day and the Pillar of fire by night.

In Deuteronomy, He is the Prophet like unto Moses.

In Joshua, He is Captain of our salvation.

In Judges, He is Judge and Lawgiver.

In Ruth, He is our kinsman Redeemer.

In 1 and 2 Samuel, He is our trusted Prophet.

In Kings and Chronicles, He is our King.

In Ezra and Nehemiah, He is the Rebuilder.

CHRIST IS ALL!

In Esther, He is our Mordecai.

In Job, He is our Everlasting Redeemer.

In Psalms, He is our Shepherd and great Theme of our song.

In Proverbs and Ecclesiastes, He is our Wisdom.

In Song of Solomon, He is our Bridegroom.

In Isaiah, He is the Prince of Peace.

In Jeremiah, He is the Righteous Branch.

In Lamentations, He is our Weeping Prophet.

In Ezekiel, He is a Heavenly Vision.

In Daniel, He is the Fourth Man in the fire.

In Hosea, He is the faithful Husband.

In Joel, He is the Baptizer with fire.

In Amos, He is our Burden-Bearer.

In Obadiah, He is the Mighty to Save.

In Jonah, He is our Great Foreign Missionary.

In Micah, He is The Messenger of Beautiful Feet.

In Nahum, He is the Avenger of God's Elect.

In Habakkuk, He is God's Evangelist.

In Zephaniah, He is our Savior.

In Haggai, He is the Restorer.

CHRIST IS ALL!

In Zechariah, He is the Fountain filled with blood.

In Malachi, He is the Sun of Righteousness with Healing in His wings.

In Matthew, He is the Messiah.

In Mark, He is the Miracle-Worker.

In Luke, He is the Son of Man.

In John, He is Son of God.

In Acts, He is the Builder of His Church.

In Romans, He is our Justifier.

In Corinthians, He is our Sanctifier.

In Galatians, He is our Redeemer from the curse of the law.

In Ephesians, He is the Christ of Unsearchable Riches.

In Philippians, He is our Great Treasure and Boast.

In Colossians, He is the fullness of the Godhead.

In Thessalonians, He is our soon-coming King.

In Timothy, He is our Mediator.

In Titus, He is our Faithful Pastor.

In Philemon, He is a Friend closer than a brother.

In Hebrews, He is our great High Priest forever.

In James, He is the Reason for good works.

In 1 and 2 Peter, He is our Shepherd.

CHRIST IS ALL!

In 1, 2, and 3 John, He is Love.

In Jude, He is coming with His saints.

In Revelation, He is the King of Kings and the Lord of Lords, the Alpha and Omega, the Beginning and the End.

He is Abel's Sacrifice, Noah's rainbow, Abraham's Ram, Isaac's Well, Jacob's ladder, Moses' Rod, Elijah's Mantle, Elisha's Staff, Gideon's Fleece, Samuel's Anointing, David's Sling, Daniel's Visions, and Malachi's Sun of Righteousness.

He is Peter's Rock, Stephen's mighty Words, Paul's blinding Light, and John's New Jerusalem.

He is Father to the orphan, Husband to the widow, Shelter to the traveler in the night; He is the bright and morning Star. To the lonesome, He is the Comforter. He is the Rose of Sharon and Water from the Rock in a "dry thirsty land."

He is the Brightness of God's glory, the Image of His Person, the King of Glory, the Pearl of Great Price, the Water in the desert, the Cup that runs over, the Staff of Comfort, and the Sustainer of life, and the Author of Salvation!

He is Jesus of Nazareth, the Son of the living God! He is not just a representative of God; He was not merely a good man that God chose; He was and is God!

He is my Savior, my Companion, my Lord and my King! At His name, "Every knee shall bow and every tongue shall confess that He is Lord."

Have you made that confession? One day you will; Scripture promises as much. Please make that confession now before it is eternally too late!

CHRIST IS ALL!

Above all, contemplate your blessed Redeemer, seated on His great white throne, encircled with heavenly glory.

Look at the King in His beauty!

It is the sight of a glorified Savior that will make the heaven of the believer.

Endeavor now, by the eye of faith, to behold the Lord Jesus in all His matchless beauty and excellence.

Contemplate His glorious character

His infinite mercy

His unparalleled condescension

and His boundless love.

There is enough in Jesus to employ the soul in rapturous meditation through a vast eternity:

His excellence, His goodness, and His love can never be fathomed.

O, then, keep your eye fixed on this adorable Savior, while you sojourn in this valley of tears; and in a little while you shall see Him as He is – face to face, and ascribe to Him unceasing praise.

David Harsha

47
THE GOSPEL OF
THE GREAT KING!

I want you to know my King! And more importantly, I want you to be known by Him. In this chapter, I've given you a brief outline of the Gospel of Jesus Christ, so that you might believe in Him if you haven't already and follow Him as your King of kings and Lord of lords. This is the best news in all the world! If you have already believed in Him, enjoy this good news again! May it never get old!

GOD: God is the King of all the world. He is the everlasting God Who has always existed as one God in three Persons Who are each fully and distinctly God: God the Father, God the Son, and God the Holy Spirit.

"Before the mountains were brought forth, or ever You had formed the earth and the world, from everlasting to everlasting You are God." Psalm 90:2

God created the world and everything in it from nothing.

"In the beginning, God created the heavens and the earth." Genesis 1:1

CHRIST IS ALL!

God is all-powerful, all-knowing, all-loving, all-merciful, all-just, all-righteous, and all-good. There is truly no one like Him!

MAN: God made man and woman in His own image.

"Then God said, 'Let Us make man in Our image, after Our likeness. And let them have dominion over the fish of the sea and over the birds of the heavens and over the livestock and over all the earth and over every creeping thing that creeps on the earth.' So God created man in His own image, in the image of God He created him; male and female He created them." Genesis 1:26-27

God created men and women to know Him in a personal relationship, to trust Him, to love Him, to delight in Him, and to obey Him. When Jesus was asked: "Which is the greatest commandment in the law?" He responded:

"You shall love the Lord your God with all your heart and with all your soul and with all your mind. This is the great and first commandment. And a second is like it: You shall love your neighbor as yourself." Matthew 22:37-39

God created us to do everything we do in such a way that we display His infinite worth and value – His glory.

"So, whether you eat or drink, or whatever you do, do all to the glory of God." 1 Corinthians 10:31

The bad news is that our first parents, Adam and Eve, and all of us after them have sinned against God. We have not trusted in God as we should. We have not loved Him as we should or delighted in Him as we should or obeyed Him as we should.

Some ways we've sinned against God by breaking His laws include: lying, stealing, disobeying parents, committing sexual sin, lusting, murdering, being angry, and mainly, we have selfishly lived for our own glory instead of God's.

The Bible describes our sinfulness this way:

"Do you not know that the unrighteous will not inherit the kingdom of God? Do not be deceived: neither the sexually immoral, nor idolaters, nor adulterers, nor men who practice homosexuality, nor thieves, nor the greedy, nor drunkards, nor revilers, nor swindlers will inherit the kingdom of God." 1 Corinthians 6:9-10

"Now the works of the flesh are evident: sexual immorality, impurity, sensuality, idolatry, sorcery, enmity, strife, jealousy, fits of anger, rivalries, dissensions, divisions, envy, drunkenness, orgies, and things like these. I warn you, as I warned you before, that those who do such things will not inherit the kingdom of God." Galatians 5:19-21

". . . for all have sinned and fall short of the glory of God" Romans 3:23

Because we have all sinned against God, and because He is a good, holy, and righteous God, He is rightfully angry at us because of our sin, and He promises to punish every unrepentant sinner in hell forever.

"You [God] Who are of purer eyes than to see evil and cannot look at wrong" Habakkuk 1:13

"For the wages of sin is death" Romans 6:23

"The LORD tests the righteous, but His soul hates the wicked and the one who loves violence. Let Him rain coals on the wicked; fire and sulfur and a scorching wind shall be the portion of their cup." Psalm 11:5-6

". . . when the Lord Jesus is revealed from heaven with His mighty angels in flaming fire, inflicting vengeance on those who do not know God and on those who do not obey the gospel of our Lord Jesus. They will suffer the punishment of eternal destruction, away from the presence of the Lord and from the glory of His might" 2 Thessalonians 1:7-9

CHRIST: But God is also a loving, merciful, and patient God, so He planned a way to remove His own anger towards sinners by sending His Son Jesus Christ into the world to save sinners.

"For God so loved the world, that He gave His only Son, that whoever believes in Him should not perish but have eternal life." John 3:16

Jesus was and is God in human flesh. He is both fully God and fully man. The Spirit calls Him the Word made flesh.

"In the beginning was the Word, and the Word was with God, and the Word was God. He was in the beginning with God. All things were made through Him, and without Him was not any thing made that was made . . . And the Word became flesh and dwelt among us, and we have seen His glory, glory as of the only Son from the Father, full of grace and truth." John 1:1-3, 14

Jesus is the only man Who never sinned. He lived a perfect life; He always glorified God perfectly; and He loved God with all His heart, mind, soul, and strength, and He loved His neighbor as Himself.

Jesus was obedient all the way to death on the cross where He, though He's the only One Who did not deserve to die and suffer, died and suffered and took the anger of God upon Himself, so that it would be removed from sinners.

"For our sake He [God the Father] made Him [Jesus – God the Son] to be sin Who knew no sin, so that in Him we might become the righteousness of God."
2 Corinthians 5:21

On the cross, Jesus paid for sins as a substitute for sinners. He did not deserve to die, but He died and absorbed the anger of God against sinners, so that sinners could be forgiven by God and yet God would still remain a righteous, just God.

"for all have sinned and fall short of the glory of God, and are justified by His grace as a gift, through the redemption that is in Christ Jesus, Whom God put forward as a propitiation by His blood, to be received by faith. This was to show God's righteousness, because in His divine forbearance He had passed over former sins. It was to show His righteousness at the present time, so that He might be just and the justifier of the one who has faith in Jesus." Romans 3:23-26

Jesus didn't stay dead, but God raised Him up from the tomb, triumphing over sin, death, and Satan as God's perfect, anger-removing sacrifice. Jesus is alive and lives forevermore to save His people from their sins!

"But on the first day of the week, at early dawn, they went to the tomb, taking the spices they had prepared. And they found the stone rolled away from the tomb, but when they went in they did not find the body of the Lord Jesus. While they were perplexed about this, behold, two men stood by them in dazzling apparel. And as they were frightened and bowed their faces to the ground, the men said to them, 'Why do you seek the living among the dead? He is not here, but has risen. Remember how He told you, while He was still in Galilee, that the Son of Man must be delivered into the hands of sinful men and be crucified and on the third day rise.' And they remembered His words"
Luke 24:1-8

RESPONSE: The benefits of what Jesus won for sinners on the cross can be yours if you repent and believe in Jesus Christ and His amazing Gospel message.

"Repent therefore, and turn again, that your sins may be blotted out" Acts 3:19

"Believe on the Lord Jesus Christ, and you will be saved" Acts 16:31

"Now to the one who works, his wages are not counted as a gift but as his due. And to the one who does not work but trusts Him Who justifies the ungodly, his faith is counted as righteousness" Romans 4:4-5

"For by grace you have been saved through faith. And this is not your own doing; it is the gift of God, not a result of works, so that no one may boast. For we are His workmanship, created in Christ Jesus for good works, which God prepared beforehand, that we should walk in them." Ephesians 2:8-10

Repentance is turning from sin in heart, mind, and action and turning to God with all your heart, mind, soul, and strength. Believing in the Lord Jesus Christ means you trust in Him as your only hope for life, joy, peace, and salvation in life, in death, and for all of eternity.

Please repent and believe today! Ask God to give you a new heart and to save you from your sins! If you do repent and believe in the Gospel, God has given you a new heart and has caused you to be born again (John 3). God's Spirit is at work in your life, and He will come and live inside of you. You will more and more hate your sin and turn from it and seek to obey and follow Jesus by the power of His Holy Spirit. If you sin, confess your sins to God, and He will be merciful to you and forgive!

"If we confess our sins, He is faithful and just to forgive us our sins and to cleanse us from all unrighteousness." 1 John 1:9

For more information about the Gospel of Jesus Christ or about how to trust and follow Him, please contact me at joseph.randall@gmail.com. Lord willing, I will try to help you find a faithful, Bible-believing church near you where you can grow in your new faith. May God work in your life and allow you to behold King Jesus in His beauty!

CHRIST IS ALL!

To learn more about the Gospel of Jesus Christ, please visit these helpful websites:

1. http://cdn.desiringgod.org/pdf/books_bfyj/bfyj.pdf

2. http://www.matthiasmedia.com.au/2wtl/

3. http://www.christianityexplored.org/what-is-christianity

4. https://www.youtube.com/watch?v=wUDgBNhKBME

How precious is Your steadfast love, O God! The children of mankind take refuge in the shadow of Your wings. They feast on the abundance of Your house, and You give them drink from the river of Your delights.

Psalm 36:7-8

As a deer pants for flowing streams, so pants my soul for You, O God. My soul thirsts for God, for the living God. When shall I come and appear before God?

Psalm 42:1-2

O God, You are my God; earnestly I seek You; my soul thirsts for You; my flesh faints for You, as in a dry and weary land where there is no water. So I have looked upon You in the sanctuary, beholding Your power and glory. Because Your steadfast love is better than life, my lips will praise You. So I will bless You as long as I live; in Your name I will lift up my hands. My soul will be satisfied as with fat and rich food, and my mouth will praise You with joyful lips . . . .

Psalm 63:1-5

48
S. M. LOCKRIDGE AND "JESUS IS LORD!"

Dr. Shadrach Meshach Lockridge will have the last word in this book as he pleads with you to behold King Jesus as your Lord and to take Him as your all in all! Dr. Lockridge preached another powerful description of Jesus called "Jesus is Lord!"[14] This meditation can also be found in written form in Dr. Lockridge's only published book:

The Challenge Of The Church, Provocative Discussions Of Vital Modern Issues

As you read, please come to Jesus and trust Him and enjoy Him as your Lord and God today – He is the greatest! And He alone will satisfy you like nothing in this world ever could!

---

14 You can listen to Dr. Lockridge's "Jesus is Lord!" here:

1. https://www.youtube.com/watch?v=JNyZ2cSFDl4

2. https://www.youtube.com/watch?v=WdGd4L6VqLo

Accessed 06 JAN 2015.

Jesus Is Lord![15]

The title Lord is a mark of respect and is an implied pledge of obedience.
Once Simon Peter stood before a hostile crowd and said: "God hath made that same Jesus Whom ye have crucified both Lord and Christ."

Christ represents the thing which God hath done to redeem us.

Lord represents that which we ought to do because we are redeemed. We ought to call Him Master and be His obedient servants!
We ought to call Him Owner because He possesses absolutely our lives!
In Him we live and move and have our being!
We ought to call Him Father and be obedient sons and daughters!
He is our only hope!
He is our only help!
God is our refuge and our strength . . .

Jesus is Lord!

He came down the stairway of heaven:
Born in Bethlehem!
Brought up in Nazareth!
Baptized in Jordan!
Tempted in the wilderness!
Performed miracles by the roadside!
Healed multitudes without medicine and made no charges for His services!
He conquered everything that came up against Him!
He even went up on Calvary and died there and then went down in the grave!

---

15 S. M. Lockridge, *The Challenge Of The Church, Provocative Discussions Of Vital Modern Issues* (Grand Rapids: Zondervan, 1969), 62-64.

CHRIST IS ALL!

And there cleaned out the grave and made it a pleasant
place to wait for the resurrection!
And then on scheduled time by the might of His own power
He got up with every form of power in the orbit of His
omnipotence!
Men have been trying to wrestle His power from Him all
these years!
Then, then they are trying to wait; they think that maybe
one time His power will fail!
Men have tried to destroy Him!
But don't you know you can't destroy Him!
What you gonna use for power – all power belongs to Him!

Well, if you try to destroy Him by fire, He'll refuse to burn!
If you try to destroy Him by water, He'll walk on the water!
If you try to destroy Him by a strong wind, the tempest will
lick His hand and lay down at His feet!
If you try to destroy Him with the Law, you'll find no fault
in Him!
If you try to destroy Him with the seal of an empire, He'll
break it!
If you try to destroy Him by putting Him in the grave, He'll
rise!
If you try to destroy Him by rejection or ignoring Him,
before you know it you'll hear a still, small voice saying
behold I stand at the door and knock!
If a man open the door I'll come in and sup with Him!

He's Lord!

Yes He is! He's Lord!

He's the Pearl from Paradise!
He's the Gem from the Glory Land!
He's the true fairest of the Jewel!
He's time's choicest Theme!
He's life's strongest Cord!
He's light's clearest Ray!
He's purity's whitest Peak!
He's glory's stateliest Summit!

CHRIST IS ALL!

He's Lord!

His name stands as a synonym for free healing, friendly
help, and full salvation!
He blessed!
His blessed name is like honey to the taste!
It's like harmony to the ear!
It's like help to the soul!
It's like hope to the heart!

I'm trying to tell you – He's Lord! Yes He is!

He is higher than the heaven of heavens!
And He's holier than the Holy of Holies!

He's Lord!

In His birth is our significance!
In His life is our example!
In His cross is our redemption!
In His resurrection is our hope!

He's Lord!

At His birth men came from the East!
At His death men came from the West!
And the East and the West met in Him!

He's Lord! Yes He is! Hallelujah! He's Lord!

And the Lord God omnipotent reigneth!

And He, yes He will! He's gonna reign, and you don't have
to worry!
There will come a time when every knee is gonna bow!
Not only at the name but to the name!
And every knee is gonna bow in the name!
What! Every knee is gonna bow and every tongue is gonna
confess!

CHRIST IS ALL!

I confess that He's my Lord!

I love to call Him my Lord!

The Lord is love!
The Lord is my light and my salvation!
The Lord is the strength of my life!
The Lord is my Shepherd I shall not want!
I shall not want for rest, for He maketh me to lie down in green pastures!
I shall not want for refreshment, for He leadeth me beside still waters!
I shall not want for forgiveness, for He restoreth my soul!
I shall not want for companionship, for yea though I walk through the valley of the shadow of death, I will fear no evil, for Thou art with me!
I shall not want for comfort, for Thy rod and Thy staff they comfort me!
I shall not want for sustenance, for Thou preparest a table before me in the presence of my enemies!
I shall not want for joy, for Thou anointest my head with oil, my cup runneth over!
I shall not want for anything in this life, for goodness and mercy shall follow me all the days of my life!
I shall not want for anything in the life to come, for I'll dwell in the house of the LORD forever!

The LORD is my Shepherd I shall not want!

The LORD is my light and my salvation!

Is He yours?!

You can crown Him King in your own heart right now!

You can crown Him Lord of all in your heart right now!

Jesus Christ is Lord!

NO KING BUT CHRIST!

Made in the USA
Columbia, SC
09 May 2020